Minds and Machines: Foundations of AI

fundae University AI, Volume 1

Viren Shah

Published by fundae University Inc, 2025.

fundae University

university.fundae.ai

Minds and Machines: Foundations and Pillars of AI

AI Foundations: Philosophy, Digital Twins, Agents & Data Engineering

By Viren Shah

Preface

We live in a time characterized by remarkable excitement around artificial intelligence, but also significant confusion about its true capabilities and limitations. Headlines regularly announce bold predictions and extraordinary promises, creating a cloud of hype that often obscures meaningful, grounded discussions about what AI truly is—and more importantly, what it can practically achieve for organizations today.

This book, *Minds and Machines: The Philosophical Foundations and Core Pillars of AI Applications*, emerges from a clear and urgent need: to cut through the noise and hyperbole surrounding artificial intelligence, providing business leaders, technical architects, and operational teams a disciplined, realistic approach to effectively harnessing AI's potential. Our aim is not to diminish enthusiasm about AI—far from it. Instead, we offer a sober, structured perspective designed explicitly to channel this enthusiasm into genuine, measurable results.

In developing this text, careful thought was given to balancing philosophical clarity with pragmatic application. Philosophy here is not an academic indulgence but a necessary anchor, firmly grounding subsequent practical implementation. By establishing clearly defined philosophical boundaries around AI, organizations can avoid the pitfalls of misplaced expectations or superficial technology deployments. A clear philosophical foundation helps distinguish between what AI genuinely can accomplish—such as automating repetitive tasks, providing reliable validation checks, and enhancing cognitive capabilities—and what it inherently cannot: replacing human empathy, creativity, or nuanced judgment.

Central to our approach is the introduction of a robust, clearly articulated three-pillar framework. This framework—comprising Data Engineering (Grounded Knowledge), AI Agents, and Human Digital Twins—translates abstract AI concepts into actionable, structured business processes. Grounded Knowledge ensures AI systems rely exclusively on meticulously prepared and semantically rich data, preventing hallucinations and inaccuracies. AI Agents streamline routine yet critical tasks, executing them with precision, consistency, and transparency. Human Digital Twins replicate structured cognitive workflows, managing routine interactions while maintaining explicit escalation pathways for complex or emotional situations. By clearly delineating roles, capabilities, and boundaries for each pillar, organizations can confidently integrate AI into their core operations.

Practicality is at the heart of this book. Throughout, readers will find detailed, real-world scenarios drawn from healthcare, pharmaceuticals, financial services, and more—illustrating precisely how these three pillars interact in practice. Structured roadmaps and a clearly outlined 90-day pilot methodology provide guidance from initial strategy to tangible results, ensuring that AI implementations deliver sustained value rather than becoming isolated technological experiments.

Ultimately, *Minds and Machines* is not another contribution to the chorus of speculative predictions about what AI might someday achieve. It is instead a disciplined, structured guide focused relentlessly on what AI can realistically deliver right now, when approached thoughtfully and methodically. Our goal is straightforward: equip you and your organization with the knowledge, frameworks, and practical tools required to navigate past the hype and genuinely realize AI's transformative promise.

Welcome to a clear-headed exploration of AI—grounded firmly in substance, disciplined execution, and measurable outcomes.

About fundae Software Inc. and fundae University

At fundae Software Inc., we believe deeply in the transformative potential of artificial intelligence—not as an abstract concept, but as a practical enabler of meaningful organizational outcomes. We have dedicated ourselves to developing innovative solutions built upon clarity, precision, and disciplined execution. Central to our approach is our proprietary, patent-pending AI agent orchestration algorithm, designed explicitly to minimize hallucinations and enhance accuracy, transparency, and reliability in AI-generated results.

fundae University is an extension of this commitment—a learning platform designed to empower individuals and organizations by sharing practical insights gained through real-world AI implementations. Rather than merely aggregating data or theoretical frameworks, the programs and content at fundae University reflect direct, hands-on experiences from fundae's ongoing work in AI-driven technologies. Our goal is to openly share the knowledge, successes, and even the challenges we've encountered, believing firmly that AI's immense potential should be accessible and clearly understood by anyone willing to engage thoughtfully.

Minds and Machines: The Philosophical Foundations and Core Pillars of AI Applications is a genuine reflection of this philosophy. It is not just another compilation of theory or abstract AI literature; rather, it embodies the actual approaches, strategic frameworks, and practical methodologies actively being developed and implemented at fundae Software Inc. Our motivation for sharing these insights is straightforward: AI has significant potential to enhance organizational efficiency and effectiveness, and we hope to help others achieve this potential through disciplined, realistic guidance drawn from genuine experience.

We are continuously learning and evolving our approach, and therefore, we actively encourage your feedback. If you find areas of the book unclear or believe there are aspects we can improve, we would greatly appreciate it if you could reach out directly to us at **fundae.university@fundae.ai**. Your input is invaluable as we strive to continuously enhance the value we deliver.

Likewise, if this book resonates positively with you and helps clarify your understanding or advance your AI initiatives, please consider sharing your experiences through a review or testimonial. Your feedback not only helps us but also supports fellow readers in making informed decisions about adopting AI in their own organizations.

Thank you for your interest, and welcome to the practical world of AI adoption with fundae.

fundae University: Professional AI Learning Tracks

1. Corporate Classroom Training: Enterprise AI Workshops

Transform your enterprise's capability through tailored, in-person workshops delivered directly at your facility. Our specialized training leverages your actual data, internal workflows, and multi-channel sales operations, ensuring immediate practical relevance. Guided by industry veterans with extensive expertise from organizations like Microsoft, AWS, and top AI startups, your teams will:

- Integrate AI solutions directly into existing contract-to-cash and sales processes
- Develop, deploy, and manage AI agents tailored for ERP, CRM, and data warehouse platforms
- Implement rigorous governance frameworks focused on compliance, safety, and cost-effectiveness

Choose from flexible formats ranging from concise two-day intensives to comprehensive five-day immersions, supported by optional ongoing mentoring and quarterly skill refreshers.

2. Virtual Instructor-Led AI Bootcamp: Intensive Weekend Cohort (3 Weeks)

Ideal for individual professionals and small teams seeking deep, structured training without travel, our immersive online bootcamp unfolds over three weekends, Saturdays and Sundays from 11 AM to 3 PM ET. Learn from seasoned professionals who bring practical enterprise AI experience into every session. You will:

- Clearly differentiate between General AI (ChatGPT, Meta, Gemini) and purpose-built Enterprise AI
- Master prompt creation and reasoning techniques essential for precise, actionable AI workflows
- Construct advanced language-model pipelines for NLP tasks, NER, Retrieval-Augmented Generation (RAG), and NLP-to-SQL
- Create sophisticated digital-twin AI agents that orchestrate multi-step processes across diverse datasets
- Apply orchestration frameworks such as LanGraph and LangChain to solve real-world challenges in healthcare, finance, logistics, and manufacturing

The USD 999 tuition includes complete session recordings, practical code notebooks, comprehensive course materials, and personalized job placement assistance. Moreover, secure employment through fundae or our extensive partner network within three months, and your tuition fee will be fully refunded.

Ready to propel your organization or career forward?

Contact us at **fundae.university@fundae.ai** for personalized corporate programs or to reserve your spot in the next virtual cohort.

Accelerate Your Enterprise Transformation with fundae's Specialized AI Solutions

At fundae Software Inc., we believe that the potential of artificial intelligence is unlocked through thoughtfully designed, expertly implemented solutions that address real-world business challenges. Alongside our commitment to education via fundae University, we provide specialized, comprehensive AI Architecture Design Services tailored explicitly to the needs of business-to-business (B2B) companies operating intricate multi-channel sales processes, particularly in the critical Contract-to-Cash (C2C) domain.

Our seasoned team of AI architects and solution designers collaborates closely with your organization's functional leaders and technical teams, bringing unmatched expertise to the design of sophisticated yet practical AI architectures. By mapping the specific nuances of your multi-channel sales processes—whether through direct sales, distribution partners, online marketplaces, or hybrid models—we help you deploy precisely tailored AI solutions that streamline complex workflows. These services are meticulously crafted to enhance revenue predictability, optimize invoicing accuracy, reduce order-to-cash cycle times, automate regulatory compliance, and significantly enhance your customer engagement experiences.

Leveraging our proprietary, patent-pending AI orchestration algorithm, our solutions dramatically reduce AI hallucinations and ensure transparent, auditable, and highly accurate results across all operational touchpoints. This ensures that your sales, finance, operations, and compliance teams can confidently depend on reliable AI-generated outcomes, freeing your workforce to focus strategically on building customer relationships, driving growth, and optimizing profitability.

Beyond our bespoke architectural design services, fundae offers an advanced, production-ready AI platform easily deployable through popular cloud providers such as Microsoft Azure and Amazon Web Services (AWS). This platform incorporates best-in-class enterprise AI capabilities, seamless integration options, robust security controls, and continuous operational reliability. With streamlined marketplace deployment, your organization can quickly leverage the powerful benefits of AI without significant upfront investment or lengthy implementation timelines.

Committed to ongoing innovation, we follow an agile, disciplined product-development cycle, delivering monthly enhancements and feature updates. These regular updates provide your organization with constant access to the latest advancements in artificial intelligence, improved system stability, expanded functionalities, and ongoing enhancements to user experience. We continuously refine our platform to meet the evolving requirements of businesses, ensuring sustained, measurable value and future-proofing your AI investments.

Choosing fundae as your AI implementation partner positions your organization to effectively navigate complexity, enhance operational excellence, and unlock strategic growth. Our holistic approach combines strategic insight, technical precision, and disciplined execution, enabling your enterprise to confidently embrace the transformative power of AI.

Join forces with fundae today, and experience firsthand how our innovative AI architecture solutions and dynamic platform capabilities can elevate your organization to the forefront of intelligent, data-driven business transformation.

To learn more about how we can help your organization transform through AI, visit us at fundae.ai or contact us at fundae.sales@fundae.ai

About the Author

Viren Shah serves as the CEO of fundae Software Inc., where he has built a reputation for weaving advanced AI solutions into existing operational systems rather than pushing companies toward major overhauls. Drawing on more than fifteen years of industry experience, he consistently favors practical strategies that reinforce an organization's strengths, believing that AI should fit naturally alongside the tools and processes already in place.

Over the course of his career, Viren has led diverse teams in applying everything from language processing and data analytics to smart automation in real-world contexts. Observing how AI initiatives often remained theoretical or disconnected from day-to-day realities, he decided to write about the methods and principles that allow enterprises to adopt AI without disrupting core operations. Through his experiences helping businesses of various sizes, he recognized the need for actionable insights that illustrate how modern AI can truly serve real-world objectives. Under Viren's leadership, fundae Software Inc. has enabled clients to balance innovation with stability, ultimately driving growth by aligning cutting-edge technology with an organization's practical demands.

Behind the Algorithm: Understanding Human Nature in Artificial Intelligence

AGI or AI Artificial General Intelligence or Artificial Intelligence is widely recognized as the newest frontier in technology, potentially redefining the interplay between humans and machines. Over recent decades, humanity has witnessed transformative technological milestones: from the widespread adoption of personal computers that democratized digital interaction, to the emergence of the World Wide Web, seamlessly connecting individuals worldwide. The advent of social media further amplified connectivity and interaction, while smartphones and tablets made powerful technology mobile and personal. Most recently, cloud computing has significantly amplified computing capacity, allowing unprecedented scalability and flexibility. Each evolutionary step has systematically empowered individuals by providing immense computational power and enhanced accessibility directly into everyday life.

Now, AGI or AI emerges as the next logical progression in this evolutionary chain. However, unlike its predecessors, AGI or AI remains conceptually fluid and inherently ambiguous, defined and perceived differently depending on one's perspective. Proponents and optimists, such as Sam Altman of OpenAI and Satya Nadella of Microsoft, advocate for AI's potential, envisioning it as a powerful force capable of catalyzing innovation, boosting productivity, and driving profound societal advancements. In contrast, more cautious observers and skeptics including cognitive scientist Gary Marcus underscore legitimate concerns, emphasizing issues surrounding ethical implications, safety risks, transparency, and the unpredictable nature of fully autonomous systems.

Ultimately, every opinion within this spectrum carries legitimacy, precisely because AGI or AI itself is continuously evolving. The only constant factor is change, change in how AI is perceived, adopted, and operationalized across diverse contexts, whether it is integrated into everyday consumer technology, educational tools, governmental infrastructure, or sophisticated enterprise processes.

In evaluating AI's role, it's crucial to revisit the fundamental purpose of technology: its ability to introduce simplicity, accuracy, and precision. These essential qualities serve as the cornerstone for reliability and efficiency, critical benchmarks against which AI's effectiveness and relevance must be measured. With this foundational clarity established, let us now critically evaluate AI against these essential criteria, determining its true capability not only as a transformative technology but also as a significant human endeavor.

AI is often misunderstood as a singular entity a neatly packaged technological system ready to provide definitive answers. In reality, AI is far more complex, nuanced, and multifaceted. To truly understand what AI does and its potential role, imagine it as residing atop a vast, intricate expanse of information, a sprawling network of knowledge so extensive and varied that we might liken it to the universe itself. Let's call this expansive, intricate knowledge repository the "Universe." Within this universe exist countless streams of information, some harmonious, others contradictory, many ambiguous, and almost all open to interpretation. These elements collectively create an immense, multidimensional landscape of understanding, where simple singularities or dualities rarely apply. Instead, what emerges is a rich state of chaotic diversity.

This inherent complexity can seem overwhelming, even chaotic, hence we term this phenomenon "Chaos in the Universe." It reflects reality itself messy, unpredictable, and yet deeply interconnected. However, within this chaos exists a profound underlying order. Each fragment of knowledge is inherently multipurpose, containing within it the capacity to inform various applications, solve numerous problems, or inspire entirely new ways of thinking. Thus, the apparent chaos is not merely disorder but the fertile ground from which purposeful outcomes arise. Let's call this meaningful structure that emerges from chaos, "Purpose in the Universe."

To better grasp this concept, consider sunlight. Its rays extend indiscriminately, nurturing plants, driving photosynthesis, and generating clean, renewable energy. A single resource yields multiple indispensable outcomes, all depending on how intelligently humanity harnesses it. Similarly, AI, with its vast and seemingly chaotic knowledge base, provides an expansive reservoir accessible to humanity. This reservoir holds immense potential that becomes actionable only through informed human intervention. Just as physical resources minerals, water, wind require expertise to harness and transform into value, AI's profound knowledge ecosystem demands human skill, insight, and creativity to unlock its fullest capabilities.

Thus, AI fulfills the foundational criteria of what any effective technology must accomplish: it places immense, previously inaccessible power into human hands. It democratizes knowledge, provides pathways toward deeper understanding, and enables solutions across diverse fields, from medicine and education to governance and enterprise efficiency. AI is not merely technology for technology's sake; rather, it embodies the promise of technology itself providing humanity with powerful tools to navigate complexity, achieve precision, and ultimately enhance our collective ability to thrive within our increasingly intricate world.

To truly grasp how AI fulfills its transformative promise, it is essential to first recognize how humanity has historically approached the task of managing knowledge. Until recently, human civilization stored information in isolated pockets each form disconnected from the others, guarded within distinct silos, often inaccessible or comprehensible only to specialized individuals. The vast knowledge of the world was fragmented, scattered across diverse mediums: pages within physical books and journals hidden away on library shelves; documents painstakingly digitized but buried within obscure databases; or structured data stored meticulously in digital archives unintelligible without advanced technical skills. Knowledge, rather than a universally available resource, became an elusive entity accessible only to those who possessed specific tools, expertise, or privileged access.

Consider the World Wide Web itself, a monumental achievement in connectivity, yet one that presented its own limitations. Algorithms like Google's PageRank dramatically improved the accessibility of information, but they were fundamentally limited these technologies indexed webpages, not genuine knowledge. Users could retrieve web documents swiftly, but extracting meaningful, structured insights still required significant cognitive and interpretive effort. Similarly, querying languages like SQL provided an effective method to pull precise fragments of structured data from large databases. However, even SQL required specialized training and a high level of technical fluency, making it accessible primarily to professionals with specific training, while remaining inaccessible to the majority.

Thus, knowledge was abundant yet perpetually incomplete. The tools at hand were powerful but imperfect; they often left gaps in understanding or demanded a specialized skill set that most people simply did not possess. The great potential of collective human wisdom remained tantalizingly close but frustratingly elusive. Knowledge was power, indeed but it remained concentrated in the hands of a relatively small number of gatekeepers, those who knew precisely how to harness and decode its complex layers.

This limitation underscores a crucial issue: knowledge, in its truest and fullest form, is most valuable when universally accessible. Just as physical resources energy, water, minerals lose potential value when restricted to only a select group of individuals, the vast reservoir of human knowledge remains underutilized if confined to niche expertise or specialized technical skills. Our capacity to innovate, to create order from chaos, and to recognize purpose in complexity becomes profoundly restricted when large segments of humanity are left unable to engage meaningfully with the vast storehouses of human understanding.

AI fundamentally disrupts this restrictive paradigm by making knowledge not only more comprehensive but profoundly accessible. Rather than merely retrieving documents or extracting isolated bits of structured information, AI has the potential to dynamically navigate the vast, chaotic complexity of available knowledge and present structured insights in formats intuitively comprehensible to anyone, irrespective of their technical proficiency. In doing so, AI promises to democratize information at an unprecedented scale, allowing each individual to construct their unique sense of order and meaning from the previously impenetrable noise of accumulated knowledge.

By embracing AI, humanity steps into a new era of knowledge democratization one where access to complex, multidimensional insights becomes universally achievable. Individuals across diverse backgrounds and skill sets can tap directly into this previously fragmented knowledge universe, harnessing its potential fully and independently. This remarkable technological shift empowers everyone not just a privileged few to navigate complexity, discover meaningful patterns within chaos, and leverage knowledge to its ultimate, purposeful potential.

AI holds the promise to usher in a new era of knowledge democratization one where access to complex, multidimensional insights could become universally achievable. Individuals across diverse backgrounds and skill sets might tap directly into this previously fragmented knowledge universe, harnessing its potential fully and independently. This remarkable technological shift offers the potential to empower everyone not just a privileged few to navigate complexity, uncover meaningful patterns within chaos, and leverage knowledge to its ultimate, purposeful potential.

Just as the universe presents an immense and intricate tapestry of resources and energies in seemingly chaotic arrangements, the landscape of human knowledge similarly exists as a dense mesh of information, vast and often bewildering in its complexity. To successfully navigate this complexity and derive meaningful order, one must first recognize and clearly identify the nature and type of knowledge available, discern its inherent purpose, and carefully align it with a clearly articulated need or goal. Consider sunlight as a resource: raw solar energy itself is abundant, yet inherently chaotic in its dispersal. Only when recognized for its specific purpose such as growing crops through photosynthesis, generating renewable electricity via photovoltaic panels, or sterilizing water using ultraviolet rays can its latent potential transform into genuine power and utility. Without clarity of purpose and precise alignment to a specific human need, sunlight remains abundant yet untapped.

Similarly, AI carries the immense promise to embed genuine cognition into technology, transforming it from a mere tool into a more intuitive medium of knowledge discovery and utilization. Historically, humanity has created impressive technological achievements, each intricately tailored to solve highly specialized challenges. For instance, advanced machine learning algorithms have been meticulously designed to optimize global food supply chains, dynamically managing distribution logistics, reducing waste, and ensuring timely delivery. Likewise, highly sophisticated software has enabled surgical robots to operate with extraordinary precision, minimizing risks and elevating medical outcomes. However, these remarkable advancements are still largely predicated upon specialized knowledge, accessible exclusively to highly skilled professionals. This exclusivity severely limits the broader accessibility of knowledge, leaving large portions of humanity disconnected from benefiting fully from these technological achievements.

Yet, despite the highly specialized nature of certain knowledge, the foundational truths underpinning that knowledge remain universal. AI offers a groundbreaking promise to bridge this gap, democratizing access to even the most complex forms of understanding. Knowledge today exists scattered across diverse mediums and formats digitally archived texts and journals, expansive libraries filled with centuries of accumulated scholarship, intricate computer code, structured databases, unstructured multimedia content, and countless other specialized resources. Currently, extracting and synthesizing information from these disparate forms requires significant effort and specialized expertise. AI promises to alleviate this fundamental limitation, integrating knowledge across multiple formats, deciphering intent and context, and seamlessly translating sophisticated information into accessible and easily comprehensible formats.

Imagine, for instance, a scenario where medical research data, stored in complex databases and encoded in specialist terminology, becomes immediately comprehensible to a rural healthcare provider without advanced training. AI, capable of understanding both the context of the information and the user's intent, could instantaneously synthesize vast amounts of specialized data, providing critical insights directly in a simplified, actionable form. Or consider a small business owner accessing global market trends: previously restricted by the technical complexities inherent in financial modeling software, AI could enable this entrepreneur to harness sophisticated economic forecasting methods without requiring expert knowledge, immediately converting complex financial information into straightforward recommendations and strategies.

This is the transformative promise that AI holds: not merely to automate or simplify tasks, but to infuse genuine cognitive capabilities into technology, enabling anyone regardless of their educational background or specialized expertise to effectively navigate the complexities of our collective knowledge. By recognizing human intent and accurately interpreting context, AI can guide individuals through chaotic informational landscapes, creating structured, purposeful order from what previously seemed impenetrable chaos. In this powerful democratization of knowledge, AI positions itself uniquely not simply as another technological innovation, but as an empowering force capable of elevating humanity's collective ability to harness the true, boundless potential embedded within the universe of knowledge itself.

As with any physical tool, technology, or resource that profoundly impacts society, the optimal utilization of AI hinges critically upon maintaining clarity about its fundamental nature and resisting narrow interpretations imposed by select perspectives. Historically, the adoption of significant innovations has often been shaped by a handful of powerful voices whose biases or agendas skew perceptions, ultimately influencing how technologies are perceived, valued, or even misrepresented. When navigating a chaotic environment whether it involves complex societal interactions, competing viewpoints, or vast realms of available information it becomes crucial not merely to identify the presence of noise but also to consciously disregard it. Noise, after all, frequently emerges not from an absence of purpose but rather from purposeful agendas or subjective interpretations that cloud objective analysis.

Thus, when confronting the multifaceted, nuanced question of AI's purpose and meaning, we must remain mindful that multiple interpretations will inevitably surface, each laden with biases, aspirations, or institutional priorities. Yet, for the practical and productive application of AI, we must simplify and concretize our understanding. AI, in this practical sense, should be perceived fundamentally as a robust, flexible framework a method for systematically extracting, synthesizing, and presenting knowledge derived from diverse sources in clear, understandable language, tailored explicitly to the user's familiarity and comfort.

To truly appreciate what AI represents, we must explicitly acknowledge what AI is not or, more accurately, to what it is not limited. AI transcends mere automation, though it indeed automates processes. AI goes beyond natural language conversational interfaces, though it masterfully engages users in fluent dialogues. AI surpasses machine learning algorithms aimed solely at prediction, estimation, or probability assessment, even though such predictive capabilities are integral parts of its structure. AI extends beyond mere code generation, though it readily crafts sophisticated software instructions. AI is more expansive than a virtual assistant for daily tasks such as travel planning or calendar management, although it performs these functions effortlessly and intuitively. Indeed, AI embodies all these capabilities collectively and yet, it remains much more expansive and powerful than the sum of these individual parts.

At its core, AI represents the incorporation of cognitive-like capabilities into computer code, enabling technology not merely to execute tasks but to intelligently comprehend the intent behind requests, establish nuanced context, discern the most appropriate and credible sources of knowledge, and dynamically generate solutions, analyses, or insights in formats explicitly tailored to the end user. It is the embedding of cognitive functionality the ability to interpret, adapt, learn, and refine understanding within digital systems that constitutes the essential "Intelligence" in Artificial Intelligence. Because these sophisticated cognitive capabilities are encoded digitally, residing in silicon chips rather than organic neurons, this intelligence is accurately labeled "artificial."

Nevertheless, it remains imperative to clearly differentiate AI from human intelligence, as the two operate in fundamentally distinct realms. Human intelligence derives its uniqueness from emotional sensitivity, intuition, situational awareness, ethical considerations, and a deep capacity for empathy and judgment. It evolves continuously, informed profoundly by context, experience, and conscious and subconscious emotional responses. In sharp contrast, AI as advanced and dynamic as it may become remains intrinsically task-oriented, defined by its initial programming, algorithms, and the data upon which it is trained. AI lacks genuine emotional or subjective awareness, operating instead within the precise boundaries of its prescribed tasks, relying solely on patterns, rules, and learned algorithms to navigate challenges. Until humanity uncovers the profoundly elusive capability to code true consciousness and authentic self-awareness into machines an achievement far beyond current or immediately foreseeable capabilities human intelligence will continue to surpass any form of artificial cognition.

Therefore, as we stand on the precipice of unprecedented technological advancement, the profound potential of AI must be embraced not with apprehension or overestimation but rather with clarity, humility, and thoughtful consideration. AI's true value lies not merely in mimicking human cognition but in complementing and amplifying it making vast troves of fragmented knowledge broadly accessible, understandable, and actionable. By maintaining a clear, practical perspective on AI's strengths, limitations, and fundamental nature, humanity positions itself not only to maximize the immense opportunities AI presents but also to navigate responsibly through the complex landscape it inevitably creates.

AI in Action: Practical Implementations Across Real-World Domains

Even though the very term Artificial Intelligence prominently features the word "Intelligence," we must remember that AI, fundamentally, remains a technological innovation. Like any technology, its meaningful integration into daily life whether in education, healthcare, enterprises, government operations, law enforcement, or everyday consumer interactions demands a structured and deliberate process. The sheer abundance of available knowledge is inherently chaotic, and to transform that chaos into meaningful order requires thoughtful, deliberate structures. Such structures should never be mere replicas of so-called "best practices" lifted from academic research papers or the latest advisory publications, regardless of their scholarly merits. Instead, an effective structure must always originate from a deep understanding of the user's specific intent, context, and purpose. What precisely does the user aim to achieve? How will the user genuinely benefit from harnessing this abundance of knowledge? These questions form the crucial foundation upon which meaningful AI implementations must rest.

Consider practical scenarios: A school district wishes to enhance student learning experiences through personalized education. AI in this context could dynamically adapt educational content based on individual student abilities, progress, and areas of difficulty, effectively transforming classrooms into personalized learning environments. Another example might involve healthcare institutions leveraging AI to interpret massive volumes of medical data, not merely to automate mundane tasks, but to offer tailored treatment recommendations that empower healthcare providers to make more accurate and timely decisions. In government services, AI-driven platforms could help policymakers rapidly distill vast quantities of economic data to anticipate and mitigate socioeconomic risks, streamlining welfare programs to deliver more targeted, responsive aid to communities in need. Similarly, in law enforcement, AI might sift through immense datasets, identifying subtle patterns to help predict, prevent, and solve crimes more efficiently. In each of these cases, the true measure of AI's value lies not in generalized solutions, but in its capacity to serve the distinct needs, contexts, and objectives of diverse users.

Every enduring structure whether physical, such as a towering skyscraper, or conceptual, like a technological system is ultimately built upon carefully designed foundations or pillars. AI is no exception. When constructing any robust system intended to endure for generations, we meticulously assess the integrity and strength of each element involved. Weaknesses must be anticipated and mitigated; risks must be clearly identified and managed. Larger environmental and societal factors are weighed thoughtfully, ensuring long-term viability and sustainability. This rigorous, comprehensive approach must apply equally to the adoption of AI. Thoughtful deployment requires carefully developed frameworks that consider immediate needs alongside long-term implications, thereby creating enduring value.

Yet, unlike static technologies, AI uniquely possesses a dynamic characteristic: it continuously learns, adapts, and evolves. This ability to learn and adjust its intrinsic capacity for iterative improvement distinguishes AI from other technologies and fundamentally alters how we must approach its implementation. This evolutionary trait means AI does not operate on any perpetual absolute truth. Unlike conventional machinery, whose functions are limited to fixed tasks defined explicitly by their initial design, AI thrives precisely because it can adapt, learning continuously from new information, interactions, and experiences. This adaptive intelligence makes AI powerful but also introduces inherent fluidity into its nature. It must be treated as a technology always in flux, continually refined, recalibrated, and guided by human oversight.

Thus, when designing AI systems for real-world application, it is essential to acknowledge this dynamic, adaptive nature. Structures built around AI must, therefore, incorporate flexibility as a foundational principle. While conventional engineering might prioritize stability above all else, AI frameworks must balance reliability with adaptability ensuring consistency without sacrificing responsiveness to evolving needs and conditions. The goal is not to eliminate uncertainty altogether, as that is impossible in the context of learning systems. Instead, the goal is to manage uncertainty responsibly, thoughtfully guiding AI's continuous evolution toward beneficial outcomes.

The ultimate promise of AI lies precisely in this balanced approach, wherein intelligent systems become trusted partners capable of enhancing human capabilities, augmenting judgment, and complementing our inherent limitations. To achieve this promise, we must construct AI foundations rooted firmly in clarity of purpose, meticulous attention to intent and context, and a profound understanding of human needs. Only through such deliberate and thoughtful structuring can AI's full potential be responsibly realized, transforming chaos into order, uncertainty into actionable intelligence, and abundant knowledge into genuine empowerment.

The successful adoption and practical application of AI demand a robust and clearly articulated foundation, purposefully designed to navigate complexity and uncertainty while consistently delivering reliable outcomes. This foundation, at its core, revolves around AI's unique ability to intuitively discern user intent, systematically establish appropriate context, intelligently extract relevant information from diverse and abundant knowledge sources, and respond meaningfully to the questions and tasks posed by users. AI, therefore, is more than simply advanced technology; it is a sophisticated approach to knowledge integration, synthesis, and delivery.

To genuinely enable such powerful capabilities, AI's foundational structure is built upon three pivotal pillars: Human Digital Twins, AI Agents, and Data Engineering. Together, these pillars provide the structural integrity, flexibility, and intelligence required for AI to transform vast, unstructured knowledge into actionable insights that humans can understand, trust, and leverage effectively.

The first pillar, Human Digital Twins, represents an advanced conceptual leap forward in digital representation. Human Digital Twins are meticulously crafted virtual replicas of real individuals, not simply digital likenesses or superficial avatars, but sophisticated entities capable of mirroring genuine human cognitive processes. These digital entities replicate the cognitive capacity to process, analyze, synthesize, and interpret knowledge with the depth and nuance approaching human cognition. However, it is critical to note that, despite their cognitive sophistication, Human Digital Twins inherently lack true emotional intuition and genuine situational awareness that humans naturally possess. Instead, they focus exclusively on knowledge-driven, contextually informed decision pathways capable of simulating intricate cognitive reasoning, pattern recognition, and knowledge interpretation, yet free from emotional biases and subjective influences. By doing so, they significantly amplify human decision capabilities without diluting the inherent authenticity and emotional intelligence of the human experience itself.

Complementing the cognitive pillar are AI Agents, representing the second foundational pillar of practical AI. AI Agents function as dedicated digital helpers, systematically conducting essential tasks that humans traditionally perform but which require little or no explicit cognitive judgment. These tasks are typically routine, repetitive, or technical yet remain fundamentally critical to efficient operation and information managing. Examples of such tasks include generating sophisticated SQL queries to mine and retrieve specific data from large databases, systematically reading through extensive documents to isolate and summarize key points or automatically indexing vast volumes of textual or numerical information. By delegating these types of tasks to AI Agents, humans are freed from mundane, repetitive duties, allowing them to focus more effectively on higher-level cognitive responsibilities. Thus, AI Agents directly increase human efficiency by streamlining and automating routine information-processing tasks, ensuring accuracy, consistency, and reliability while preserving human cognitive resources for tasks genuinely requiring nuanced judgment, emotional intelligence, and situational awareness.

The third critical pillar of AI's foundational structure is Data Engineering. Effective AI implementation depends profoundly upon the strategic organization and structuring of information transforming vast and chaotic datasets into structured, coherent, and AI-accessible knowledge. Data Engineering accomplishes precisely this transformation, creating a unified and clearly navigable information landscape through comprehensive data structuring and meticulous metadata tagging. This AI-readable metadata framework enables AI systems to rapidly and accurately locate, interpret, and synthesize relevant data points, thus delivering targeted, contextually accurate, and meaningful insights to users. Without rigorous Data Engineering, AI systems become overwhelmed by raw information abundance, failing to translate data into reliable, actionable knowledge. Consequently, sophisticated Data Engineering is vital, functioning as the guiding map that enables AI models to traverse vast knowledge oceans efficiently, reliably, and purposefully.

While these three pillars Human Digital Twins, AI Agents, and Data Engineering each provide distinct foundational support, their true power emerges precisely because they function not as separate, isolated components, but as integral parts of a single, unified, and mutually reinforcing framework. The efficacy of AI applications hinges fundamentally upon their cohesive integration. Omitting or neglecting any one of these pillars inherently compromises the effectiveness, completeness, and reliability of the entire AI structure, resulting in fragmented, limited, or incomplete outcomes.

Ultimately, we adopt and integrate AI into everyday human contexts precisely because it offers an unprecedented opportunity to transform chaotic, abundant knowledge into structured, purposeful, and accessible insights. AI's foundational pillars allow it not only to understand the nuanced intent behind user requests but also to interpret subtle contexts and extract precise information tailored explicitly to each unique scenario. By deliberately building AI frameworks around these foundational pillars, we empower ourselves to leverage AI effectively turning vast, overwhelming complexity into intuitive clarity, abundant information into actionable insights, and raw potential into genuine human empowerment.

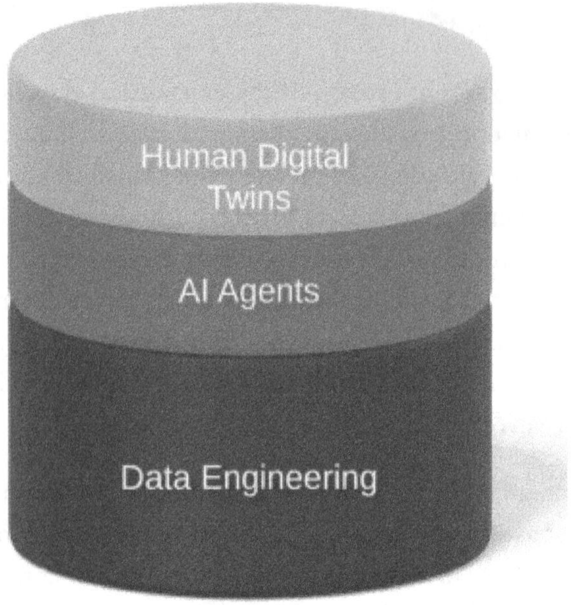

Practical AI

While the three foundational pillars Human Digital Twins, AI Agents, and Data Engineering are deeply interconnected parts of a singular, coherent AI framework, it is essential to recognize that each pillar demands a distinct and varied effort. The complexity, focus, and significance of tasks within these pillars differ fundamentally, each contributing uniquely to the overall integrity and effectiveness of practical AI applications.

Foremost among these tasks and arguably the most critical and challenging is the meticulous collation and structuring of knowledge into a coherent and consistent format. Modern large language models (LLMs) and advanced AI systems have successfully compiled and assimilated vast expanses of global knowledge, capabilities, and skills. Yet, this comprehensive aggregation remains inherently chaotic rich in information but lacking the unique, nuanced contexts essential for precise, targeted AI applications. To address this crucial gap, the knowledge required for a specific application must be carefully and intentionally organized within a dedicated knowledge repository. This deliberate structuring is known as "Grounding of Knowledge," and the carefully curated repository thus formed is termed "Grounded Knowledge." This grounding process transforms general, chaotic knowledge into structured, contextual information specifically aligned to the user's intent and the application's objectives. Without this foundational process, AI applications frequently become prone to inaccuracies, inconsistencies, and unreliable outcomes commonly referred to as "hallucinations."

Grounding of Knowledge is thus the foundational base upon which the entire AI framework is constructed. This task often demands substantial effort, precision, and careful attention to detail, representing the most resource-intensive and time-consuming phase of any AI application development. By ensuring knowledge is effectively grounded, we significantly reduce ambiguity, dramatically enhance accuracy, and establish reliability and consistency across AI interactions.

Once the grounding of knowledge is meticulously accomplished, the next essential stage in building the practical AI framework involves creating specialized AI Agents. These agents are designed explicitly to perform tasks at speeds and efficiencies far exceeding human capabilities. For instance, AI Agents can rapidly write complex code, swiftly analyze documents, or effortlessly perform data queries processes which humans would find tedious, repetitive, or prohibitively time-consuming. Consider document scanning: an AI Agent can methodically analyze a 1,000-page technical or legal document within mere minutes, identifying key points, summarizing critical details, and categorizing essential information. For a human, this task would be impractically time-consuming, taxing, and prone to errors. AI Agents alleviate these burdens dramatically, efficiently managing routine data-intensive tasks while allowing humans to dedicate their energy toward higher-order decision-making activities.

Yet, creating effective AI Agents involves more than merely instructing them on routine coding or scanning operations. The true strength and value of AI Agents come from carefully training them to navigate specific data environments, clearly identifying appropriate data stores whether file-based repositories, vector databases, data lakes, or structured data warehouses. This training also encompasses precise instructions on recognizing relevant data elements, accurately joining disparate data sources, and performing specific analytical tasks such as regression analyses, data distributions, or pattern detection. These agents become skilled navigators within a complex landscape of structured and unstructured information, capable of reliably executing predefined tasks with minimal human intervention.

Following the establishment of grounded knowledge and efficient AI Agents, the final yet crucial step in constructing the complete AI edifice involves the creation of Human Digital Twins advanced virtual representations of human roles, skillsets, and cognitive functions. These digital twins closely replicate the cognitive competencies of roles such as Data Analysts, Financial Analysts, Payroll Specialists, and various other knowledge-driven professions. Unlike AI Agents, whose strengths lie primarily in repetitive, data-centric tasks, Human Digital Twins are imbued with advanced cognitive frameworks mirroring the nuanced, knowledge-intensive, and process-oriented tasks typically managed by skilled human professionals.

For instance, a Human Digital Twin replicating a Payroll Specialist's role would manage tasks such as diagnosing payroll discrepancies with remarkable accuracy. Upon detecting irregularities, it would invoke appropriate AI Agents to swiftly extract necessary data, analyze historical payroll records, and formulate potential resolutions. However, if the situation requires nuanced emotional judgment or complex human interaction for instance, resolving disputes or managing sensitive employee relations the Digital Twin seamlessly escalates the matter to a human counterpart, recognizing the inherent limitations of its cognitive model. Similarly, a Data Analyst's Human Digital Twin could intelligently evaluate the potential financial impacts of mergers and acquisitions, performing intricate scenario analysis between two major customers. By rapidly gathering relevant data points, applying sophisticated analytical frameworks, and summarizing outcomes in clear language, this twin provides actionable insights while freeing human analysts to focus on deeper strategic considerations and nuanced decision-making.

Ultimately, the true strength of practical AI applications emerges from the deliberate, harmonious integration of these three interconnected pillars. Grounding Knowledge ensures accuracy and contextual relevance; AI Agents amplify productivity by automating routine yet critical tasks; and Human Digital Twins introduce sophisticated cognitive processing to complex, nuanced roles. Only by systematically addressing each pillar, understanding their unique demands and capabilities, and weaving them cohesively together can organizations build robust, sustainable AI systems. Such systems transcend mere technological innovation, becoming invaluable strategic resources efficiently transforming vast, chaotic information into reliable, actionable knowledge capable of empowering human potential.

With this comprehensive understanding of the interconnected nature of AI's foundational pillars, it becomes clear that a deeper exploration into each pillar is essential to grasp how AI truly functions in practical scenarios. To begin, it is logical to focus first on Data Engineering, as this forms the foundational bedrock of any AI application. Data Engineering involves the critical task of transforming abundant yet chaotic information into structured, coherent, and actionable data sets. Only through meticulous data engineering can we create a stable and reliable knowledge framework that supports every subsequent step ensuring AI Agents and Human Digital Twins operate effectively, accurately, and consistently.

Structuring Chaos: The Role of Data Engineering in Building Reliable AI Foundations

Data Engineering, also known as Grounding of Knowledge, is the foundational bedrock critical to effective AI implementation. Without a meticulously grounded knowledge base, even the most advanced AI systems remain susceptible to inaccuracies, unreliable responses, and the phenomenon commonly termed AI hallucinations. Grounding of Knowledge transforms vast, disordered data into structured and contextually relevant information, empowering AI models to deliver precise and meaningful outcomes. This pivotal process revolves around carefully curating three fundamental data types Structured Data, Documents, and News Feeds. Structured Data is organized into clearly defined categories and fields, ideal for precise querying and detailed analysis. Documents encompass unstructured text such as contracts, research papers, or technical manuals, which AI must parse to extract nuanced insights. Finally, News Feeds provide a continuous stream of timely information, essential for AI to maintain contextual relevance and responsiveness. Together, these data forms, when systematically engineered, create a cohesive, reliable foundation indispensable for high-performance AI applications.

Data Engineering is not merely about collecting and storing vast amounts of data; it involves the thoughtful transformation of data into an AI-readable format that accurately captures both intent and context. Structured Data provides AI with explicit, categorized information that can be efficiently queried for precise analysis, such as financial records, customer databases, or inventory management systems. Documents, by contrast, contain nuanced, unstructured narratives contracts, manuals, and reports that demand advanced parsing techniques for meaningful interpretation. Lastly, News Feeds inject timely, dynamic, and evolving context into AI systems, ensuring responses remain current, relevant, and accurately reflective of real-world events. Without carefully engineering and integrating these three distinct yet complementary data sources, AI remains fundamentally limited, prone to errors and unable to achieve true contextual understanding. Effective grounding thus becomes the crucial step to unlocking AI's full potential, turning scattered knowledge into actionable, trustworthy intelligence.

Knowledge or information, whether consumed by individuals, organizations, or governments, exists across numerous formats each carrying distinct characteristics and levels of accessibility. Among these, the most common and systematically organized is structured data, frequently considered the primary knowledge source due to its inherent clarity, consistency, and ease of use. For individuals, structured data underpins daily interactions via user-friendly apps like online banking platforms, where account balances, transaction histories, and financial trends are clearly organized and readily accessible. Similarly, travel booking apps utilize structured data, making flight schedules, hotel availability, and pricing details easily retrievable, providing immediate insights and facilitating seamless decisions.

For organizations and governments, the value of structured data multiplies exponentially, serving as the backbone of their operational efficiencies and strategic decision-making processes. Businesses meticulously categorize customer data, financial transactions, supply-chain details, employee records, and inventory management information within structured repositories such as relational database management systems (RDBMS), comprehensive data warehouses, and expansive data lakes. This clear, organized approach enables swift analysis, targeted queries, accurate forecasting, and efficient operational oversight. Governments similarly leverage structured data extensively, organizing vast quantities of citizen information, taxation details, public healthcare records, infrastructure data, and national census statistics each carefully cataloged to ensure ease of retrieval, robust analytics, informed policymaking, and precise governance.

In contrast to structured data, the second essential form of information document-based knowledge presents a fundamentally different challenge. Documents, though rich with critical details and comprehensive context, remain predominantly unstructured, encompassing content such as legal contracts, detailed research papers, internal policies, standard operating procedures, legislative texts, and regulatory compliance frameworks. Additionally, organizations regularly produce strategic planning documents, comprehensive audit reports, operational manuals, technical specifications, and minutes from critical meetings each containing vast amounts of valuable but loosely formatted insights. Similarly, governments rely on extensive documentation, including legal statutes, regulatory filings, white papers, environmental impact assessments, policy directives, and inter-agency communications. At the individual level, documents might include property records, insurance policies, wills, or employment contracts.

However, extracting actionable intelligence from documents remains historically cumbersome, hindered by varying authorial styles, the absence of uniform formatting, and the regulatory language that often necessitates specialized interpretation. This inherent complexity demands significant manual intervention, slowing decision-making processes and limiting immediate accessibility. The potential of such rich knowledge reservoirs remains largely untapped unless structured through advanced technologies capable of accurately interpreting nuance, context, and semantic intent.

While structured data and documents largely encapsulate historical events, interactions, and transactions, an increasingly significant third form of knowledge news feeds offers immediacy, capturing dynamic, real-time developments crucial for anticipating future conditions. News feeds provide continuously updated streams of current events, market trends, geopolitical shifts, economic announcements, weather developments, and public sentiment each profoundly influencing both short-term actions and strategic, forward-looking decisions. For individuals, news feeds have become critical for day-to-day decisions such as investment management, where real-time market updates significantly influence personal financial choices and portfolio adjustments.

Organizations increasingly depend on news feeds to manage volatility and adapt rapidly to shifting external conditions. Financial institutions monitor global economic news closely, responding swiftly to central bank announcements, policy changes, or unexpected market disruptions. Similarly, global supply-chain firms continuously track news relating to logistical bottlenecks, trade disputes, or regulatory developments, enabling them to proactively mitigate potential disruptions or swiftly capitalize on emerging opportunities. Governments, too, rely on real-time news feeds to address emerging public safety threats, swiftly respond to natural disasters, anticipate socio-political unrest, or adjust diplomatic strategies based on evolving international relations.

To fully appreciate the critical importance of news feeds, consider a specific scenario involving international tariffs. Structured data and historical documents can clearly outline previous tariff structures, trade volumes, historical market performance, and past regulatory frameworks. However, when faced with sudden policy announcements such as a government's unexpected decision to implement new tariffs or adjust existing trade agreements structured, and document-based historical data alone cannot adequately address critical "what if" scenarios. Organizations dependent solely on historical records may find themselves unprepared for such sudden economic shifts, unable to accurately assess immediate impacts or strategically reposition themselves effectively. Here, real-time news feeds become indispensable, enabling rapid response and strategic scenario planning. A manufacturing firm receiving instant notification of new tariff announcements through news feeds can swiftly evaluate immediate market implications, recalibrate procurement strategies, and dynamically adjust pricing models actions unattainable relying solely on structured historical data or document archives.

However, it is imperative to recognize these three data sources structured data, document-based knowledge, and news feeds as deeply interconnected, collectively forming a complex ecosystem of dispersed yet interdependent knowledge.

None exist independently or exclusively; instead, their true value emerges when thoughtfully integrated and systematically aligned within clear boundaries. Effective grounding of knowledge, therefore, becomes the critical process of establishing deliberate, intentional constraints on information accessibility, defining clearly what can and cannot be retrieved by AI systems. Without such strategic grounding, AI risks producing fragmented, unreliable, or contextually inappropriate insights, undermining its inherent promise.

In constructing meaningful AI applications whether for personal, organizational, or governmental use grounding knowledge across structured data, documents, and news feeds becomes a foundational imperative. It ensures coherent, context-aware insights, enabling AI to fulfill its true potential: transforming dispersed, chaotic information into clear, purposeful, and actionable information.

Though each of these three data sources Structured Data, Documents, and News Feeds possesses significant intrinsic value, their integration remains inherently complex due to their fundamentally different structures, granularity, and formatting. At their core, these data sources share only a loose, often tenuous connection, presenting considerable challenges for traditional technologies and conventional data processing methods. Each type of data is inherently specialized, maintained in separate environments, and accessed through distinctly different methodologies. Structured data typically resides in carefully organized relational databases and data warehouses, stored in rigidly defined schemas and tables. This structured environment facilitates precise querying and rapid retrieval but imposes limitations on flexibility, making any alterations or expansions highly resource intensive. A seemingly minor modification in data structures like adding a new field or changing categorization schemes necessitates extensive re-engineering, often affecting downstream applications and processes significantly.

In stark contrast, documents present a markedly different set of challenges. They contain extensive narratives, complex paragraphs, nuanced language, specialized terminology, and often comply with stringent regulatory formats, each varying widely depending on the author or institution responsible for their creation. Unlike structured databases, documents lack uniform schemas or clearly defined data points, making traditional data extraction painstaking and labor-intensive. Extracting meaningful and accurate information demands significant human effort, highly specialized linguistic and analytical skills, and comprehensive knowledge of domain-specific contexts. Even minor updates, policy revisions, or regulatory adjustments within documents typically require extensive reviews and manual reprocessing, significantly slowing responsiveness and increasing maintenance complexity.

News feeds, representing yet another data dimension, introduce real-time dynamism and continuous volatility. Unlike static documents or predictable structured databases, news feeds fluctuate unpredictably frequently changing, continuously updated, and delivered in varying formats and speeds from diverse, external sources. Integrating real-time news data into existing structured systems or document-based workflows demands sophisticated capabilities advanced data integration frameworks, specialized extraction algorithms, continuous monitoring mechanisms, and rapid-response protocols none of which traditional systems manage easily or efficiently. Any substantial development or implementation of such systems demands significant ongoing investment, not only financially but also in the highly specialized skillsets required to maintain, update, and manage the sophisticated technical infrastructure.

These complexities have historically restricted effective data integration to large organizations and governmental bodies capable of affording extensive technical resources and specialized personnel. Smaller organizations, educational institutions, local governments, and mid-sized enterprises across various sectors, despite confronting identical information integration challenges frequently lack the financial means or specialized expertise required to bridge these gaps. Consequently, they remain excluded from fully leveraging comprehensive data integration strategies, despite equally critical needs. Individuals, perhaps most notably, remain largely underserved in accessing sophisticated, personalized solutions, confined to basic services or simplistic consumer applications such as banking apps or basic booking platforms.

Yet individuals, paradoxically, stand to gain immensely from integrated data solutions. Consider, for example, students who struggle to grasp complex academic concepts. If empowered by a well-grounded knowledge integration solution, they could instantly access a diverse array of teaching methodologies from around the globe, providing different explanatory styles and approaches to learning the same topic. Similarly, an individual patient researching complex medical treatments could rapidly aggregate reliable insights from structured medical databases, patient-care documents, and recent scientific discoveries disseminated through specialized news feeds, thus empowering informed, personalized medical decisions previously accessible only through specialist consultations.

Grounding knowledge structuring, standardizing, and normalizing data across these disparate sources therefore becomes absolutely critical before any effective application, AI-based or otherwise, can reliably function. The credibility, effectiveness, and long-term adoption of any technological solution fundamentally depend on the trustworthiness and integrity of the underlying knowledge store it accesses. If users cannot rely upon the accuracy, completeness, and consistency of integrated data, the application itself becomes compromised, risking loss of trust, diminished adoption, and potentially serious decision-making errors.

This necessity underscores the essential requirement to carefully standardize and normalize information from structured data, documents, and news feeds into unified, reliable, and easily accessible repositories. Grounding knowledge systematically achieves precisely this integration, creating a cohesive, trustworthy foundation accessible by AI-driven and traditional applications alike. Without this deliberate grounding process, organizations and individuals alike remain trapped within isolated data silos, missing out on profound potential insights that integrated data could provide.

Ultimately, the careful grounding of knowledge across these diverse formats structured databases, complex documents, and rapidly changing news feeds is not simply a beneficial step but an indispensable prerequisite. It lays the groundwork for high-performance, adaptable, and reliable solutions accessible to users across diverse sectors and contexts, enabling not only large organizations but also smaller enterprises, educational institutions, local governments, and individuals to fully harness the power of integrated knowledge. Through meticulous grounding, users finally achieve meaningful

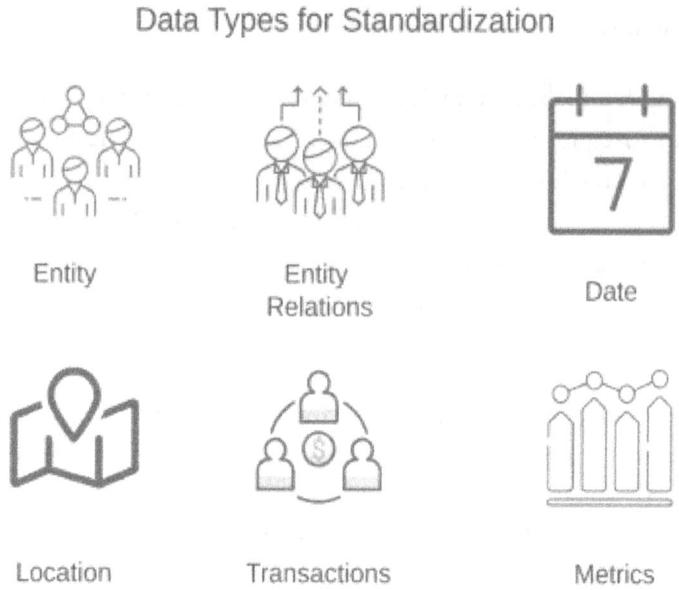

and reliable insights, transforming dispersed, chaotic information into actionable intelligence and genuine empowerment.

When discussing standardization and normalization, our structured-data-oriented mindset typically gravitates toward classical database principles such as the Third Normal Form (3NF). The concept of 3NF fundamentally pertains only to structured data contexts, specifically relational databases, where its primary purpose is to systematically reduce redundancy and dependency within data tables. This method ensures database consistency, reliability, and integrity by clearly isolating relationships, eliminating duplicate entries, and streamlining the storage and retrieval process. However, while extremely effective for structured data, 3NF falls short in addressing the inherent complexity and unstructured nature found in documents and news feeds, making it unsuitable as a universal normalization standard for creating an integrated knowledge store.

To effectively establish a genuinely grounded knowledge repository capable of integrating all three disparate data formats Structured Data, Documents, and News Feeds it becomes imperative to normalize and standardize information at a more fundamental and universally applicable level. This process involves clearly defining, categorizing, and standardizing across six primary dimensions: Entities, Entity Relations, Locations, Transactions, Dates, and Metrics.

Entities form the foundational dimension in this normalization process, encompassing both human and non-human types. Human entities represent individuals such as customers, employees, regulators, and suppliers, while non-human entities include organizations, products, assets, legal entities, intellectual property, and business units. For instance, humans can range from an individual consumer browsing an e-commerce website to a compliance officer responsible for regulatory oversight. Non-human examples include corporations like Apple Inc., specific products such as iPhones, or legal authorities like the SEC. Precisely defining these entities allows subsequent data managing and querying to become uniform, intuitive, and coherent.

Next, Entity Relations describe the interconnections among various entities. These relationships are pivotal in capturing interactions and dependencies accurately. Relationships can exist in multiple forms, such as hierarchical parent-child structures exemplified by a multinational corporation and its subsidiary units or departments, customer-supplier relationships highlighting procurement dynamics, or complex partnership agreements between distinct organizations. Additional examples include human-to-human interactions (employee-supervisor, physician-patient, advisor-client), human-to-non-human interactions (investor-stock, author-book, technician-machinery), and non-human-to-non-human relationships (company-subsidiary, product-brand, regulatory-agency-documentation). Clearly identifying these relational structures is essential in facilitating accurate data integration, interpretation, and meaningful querying.

Locations represent the geographic dimension, capturing the critical spatial context where entities reside or interact. In a globalized business environment, precise location information is increasingly significant for multiple reasons, including regulatory compliance, tax jurisdiction determination, logistical optimization, risk management, and strategic market positioning. Entities' geographic locations directly influence decisions related to trade policies, tariffs, localized marketing strategies, and supply chain configurations. For instance, understanding a manufacturing facility's location in China versus Mexico can significantly alter an organization's tariff exposure or logistical planning.

Transactions represent activities occurring between entities, capturing explicit actions such as sales, purchases, loan issuance, payments, contracts, employment agreements, settlements, leases, mergers and acquisitions, license agreements, product recalls, returns, customer service interactions, and regulatory compliance filings. Transactions thus encompass a broad spectrum of business, governmental, and personal interactions, making their accurate categorization and standardization critical for analyzing trends, forecasting outcomes, and managing processes effectively.

Dates provide the essential chronological framework for these transactions, enabling users to query, analyze, and compare activities over specific timeframes. Examples include transaction dates, effective dates of contracts, fiscal quarters, year-to-date (YTD) periods, policy implementation dates, and deadlines for regulatory compliance. Accurate date standardization allows businesses and governments to precisely analyze historical trends, anticipate cyclical events, project future outcomes, and respond proactively to market shifts or regulatory changes.

Metrics represent numerical values derived from transactions and serve as quantitative indicators of performance, impact, or trends. They range from simple metrics such as sums, counts, averages, minimums, and maximums, to more complex calculations like market share, rank, percentiles, and customer lifetime value (CLV). Additionally, longitudinal metrics such as year-over-year (YoY) growth, quarter-over-quarter (QoQ) comparisons, cumulative annual growth rate (CAGR), and period-over-period (PoP) shifts provide essential insight into longer-term performance trajectories, enabling sophisticated analyses of business effectiveness, market dynamics, and strategic outcomes.

For example, standardized metrics allow retail companies to quickly evaluate product performance by tracking average monthly sales volumes, market share positions, and year-over-year revenue growth. Similarly, healthcare organizations utilize standardized metrics such as patient readmission rates, treatment efficacy scores, and quarterly operational costs to improve outcomes. Financial institutions leverage standardized metrics like customer creditworthiness ratings, portfolio returns, and QoQ growth in managed assets to inform investment decisions. Governments utilize employment rates, inflation indices, GDP growth rates, and comparative rankings against other nations as key standardized metrics for policy decisions.

Because the original data resides in fundamentally distinct formats structured databases with rigid schemas, free-form textual documents with variable language styles, and constantly evolving, real-time news feeds achieving uniformity and consistency across these six dimensions becomes exceedingly challenging. Each format demands distinct normalization and extraction methodologies. Structured data, for instance, typically comes predefined, requiring less semantic interpretation but substantial schema maintenance. Conversely, documents demand advanced natural language processing (NLP) capabilities to extract relevant entities, relationships, and contexts accurately. News feeds, volatile and unstructured, demand sophisticated real-time normalization capabilities, rapid entity recognition, and sentiment or context interpretation.

Given these disparities, the normalization effort becomes foundationally critical. Effective grounding of knowledge involves meticulously standardizing and normalizing each dimension Entities, Entity Relations, Locations, Transactions, Dates, and Metrics to create a unified and coherent knowledge framework. Such comprehensive normalization enables seamless integration across structured data, document repositories, and news feeds. Once standardized, the integrated knowledge base becomes reliably query able, intuitively accessible, and universally trusted.

Ultimately, careful and deliberate normalization at this foundational level serves as a necessary prerequisite for integrating and leveraging disparate knowledge sources effectively. Without such normalization, the integration effort risks being fragmented, inefficient, or inaccurate undermining the credibility, reliability, and practical utility of the resulting knowledge store. Conversely, systematic normalization empowers organizations and individuals alike, providing universal access to coherent, actionable insights transforming chaotic information into strategic intelligence capable of driving informed decisions, proactive responses, and meaningful outcomes.

Now let's explore realistic business scenarios to illustrate how complex interactions in a healthcare environment can be systematically broken down into foundational data categories. By examining these simulated real-life scenarios, we gain insight into how ongoing business events, transactions, and relationships must be structured clearly to create an effective and grounded knowledge store. The following scenario will serve as our foundational context for subsequent examples:

- **Robert Wood Johnson (RWJ)** is an Integrated Delivery Network (IDN) operating under a corporate parent structure, managing multiple hospitals and clinics across various locations in New Jersey.
- Certain RWJ hospitals and clinics possess **340B-covered entity** status, qualifying them for significant pharmaceutical and medical device discounts under the Public Health Service (PHS) program.
- RWJ delivers comprehensive medical care covering virtually every therapeutic area, purchasing pharmaceuticals from various Pharma and Biotech manufacturers and acquiring medical devices from diverse device manufacturers.
- RWJ receives reimbursements for medical treatments, pharmaceuticals, and devices from several payers, including **United Health Care, Aetna, Cigna, State Medicaid, and Medicare**, each payer representing distinct reimbursement channels.
- RWJ maintains contracts with Pharma, Biotech, and Medical Device manufacturers, who provide channel-specific discounts distributed through chargebacks, rebates, and administrative fees.
- RWJ actively participates in clinical research alongside Pharma and Biotech manufacturers, research institutions, and governmental entities, and regularly publishes research outcomes, adverse events, policies, treatment guidelines, and formulary updates across platforms like clinical.doc, PubMed, NIH, RWJ portal, and press releases.
- RWJ continuously monitors regulatory guidelines issued by Federal, State, and Local governments to ensure ongoing compliance and adapt quickly to policy changes.
- Pharma, Biotech, and Medical Device manufacturers operate globally, maintaining regulatory compliance with numerous international governmental agencies, and independently publishing their own clinical research, treatment guidelines, Real-World Evidence (RWE), Health Economics Outcomes Research (HEOR) data, and press announcements.
- Within the manufacturer ecosystem, RWJ can serve multiple roles simultaneously:
    - As a **corporate parent** entity with which all financial contracts are executed, payments processed, and discounts managed.
    - As a **hospital or clinic** location where pharmaceuticals or medical devices are physically shipped, though no direct financial transactions occur at these locations.
    - As a **research partner and Key Opinion Leader (KOL)** collaborating on significant clinical and medical research initiatives.
- RWJ employs a diverse workforce, including:
    - **Medical professionals** such as doctors, nurses, and therapists who actively engage in clinical treatments and research.
    - **Non-medical professionals** including administrative staff, warehouse personnel, and financial experts who facilitate operational efficiency.
- Doctors at RWJ frequently participate in research and may also function as KOLs representing the hospital's expertise and reputation within the medical community.
- RWJ provides care to patients treated both as **inpatients and outpatients**, maintaining highly sensitive Personal Identifiable Information (PII), subject to stringent regulatory compliance regarding patient privacy and data protection.

This comprehensive scenario forms the foundation upon which specific examples illustrating the necessity of structured and grounded knowledge will be developed, highlighting how business events must be systematically categorized into clearly defined data types to effectively leverage AI-driven knowledge management.

Now let's explore another comprehensive business scenario involving a global financial institution operating at significant scale. This scenario illustrates the depth and complexity required when structuring and grounding financial and transactional knowledge across diverse geographical regions, regulatory landscapes, and financial sectors. The scenario outlined below will serve as a foundational context for subsequent detailed examples of structured knowledge management in banking:

- **United Bank** is a leading global financial services provider headquartered in the United States, operating extensively in multiple regions including North America, South America, the European Union (EU), non-EU European countries, South Africa, Middle East, India, Japan, Australia and New Zealand (ANZ), and South Korea, spanning operations across a total of 90 countries.
- The bank's service offerings include:
    - **Personal Banking**, such as checking and savings accounts, debit and credit cards, online banking services, and retirement planning.
    - **Consumer Finance**, providing various loan products, including automobile financing, home loans, mortgages, student loans, and personal loans tailored to diverse customer demographics.
    - **Corporate Banking**, delivering comprehensive services to corporate clients such as credit facilities, treasury management, trade finance, commercial lending, and syndicated loan arrangements.
    - **Investment Banking**, involving mergers and acquisitions (M&A), Initial Public Offerings (IPOs), underwriting services, securities trading, wealth management, and strategic advisory services.
    - **Foreign Investment**, managing international investments, currency exchange services, cross-border asset management, and providing regulatory guidance for clients investing in foreign markets.
- Due to its multinational presence, United Bank operates in a multi-currency environment, managing financial transactions in USD, EUR, GBP, CHF, JPY, INR, AUD, BRL, KRW, and numerous other global currencies, requiring advanced foreign exchange risk management and regulatory compliance strategies.
- United Bank engages closely with various stakeholders, including individual customers, institutional investors, regulatory bodies, central banks, and global financial markets, each representing distinct relationships and transaction types.
- The bank maintains sophisticated financial and customer data infrastructures housed in relational databases, data warehouses, and data lakes. These structured repositories store extensive customer account information, financial transaction histories, risk profiles, credit ratings, portfolio holdings, compliance audits, and transaction settlements.
- United Bank is subject to rigorous regulatory oversight, including but not limited to compliance with U.S. regulations (Federal Reserve guidelines, SEC regulations, FDIC policies, OCC standards), the European Union's regulatory frameworks (MiFID II, GDPR compliance, Basel III/IV capital adequacy norms), and equivalent financial and privacy regulations in South America, Asia-Pacific, South Africa, and Middle Eastern jurisdictions.
- The bank regularly publishes internal research, economic forecasts, market analyses, risk assessments, regulatory updates, and compliance guidelines. These publications are disseminated through various channels such as Bloomberg terminals, internal research portals, financial news websites, regulatory databases, and industry newsletters.
- As a participant in global financial markets, United Bank closely monitors ongoing geopolitical developments, economic policies, trade agreements, sanctions, and tariffs, integrating real-time insights from news feeds, press releases, financial news aggregators, and regulatory announcements to inform strategic

decision-making and risk management practices.

- Within the financial ecosystem, United Bank fulfills multiple concurrent roles:
    - As a **corporate parent**, it oversees global strategic operations, executes global financial agreements, manages corporate-level compliance, and centralizes capital allocation and risk management.
    - As a **regional or local bank entity**, United Bank directly serves local customers, providing banking services, managing daily customer interactions, and executing regional transactions, though major financial activities and strategic decisions are coordinated through the corporate parent.
    - As an **investment and advisory partner**, it engages extensively in M&A activities, financial market analyses, and complex financial restructuring efforts for its corporate clients globally.
- United Bank employs a diverse global workforce, categorized as follows:
    - **Financial Professionals**, including investment bankers, financial analysts, portfolio managers, economists, traders, risk management specialists, compliance officers, and wealth management advisors.
    - **Operational and Administrative Staff**, comprising customer service personnel, technology specialists, cybersecurity analysts, HR professionals, accounting and financial controllers, regulatory specialists, and administrative support staff.
- Bank professionals participate extensively in global economic forums, financial research conferences, regulatory consultations, and strategic market analyses, serving as key opinion leaders (KOLs) representing the bank's expertise in global finance.
- United Bank provides services to both individual and corporate clients, maintaining sensitive and personally identifiable information (PII), transactional details, risk assessments, and confidential investment data. Rigorous adherence to global standards for data security, privacy laws, financial transparency, and compliance is mandatory.

This comprehensive financial services scenario creates a clear foundation upon which structured knowledge examples will be developed, demonstrating how specific banking events, interactions, and transactional complexities must be systematically categorized into precisely defined data types to enable effective, accurate, and actionable knowledge management.

If RWJ Healthcare, pharmaceutical and medical device manufacturers, and a global financial institution such as United Bank were to develop a cross-functional NLP-based AI interface, the foundational necessity would be to effectively ground the disparate knowledge sources. Such an AI interface would need to integrate and deliver accurate, meaningful, and timely insights across various functional domains clinical operations, regulatory compliance, global manufacturing, finance, customer service, and strategic planning. RWJ would leverage NLP for patient treatment inquiries, compliance tracking, or payer negotiations; drug and device manufacturers would utilize NLP for global regulatory oversight, clinical trial monitoring, or contract analytics; and United Bank would apply NLP to global investment management, risk assessment, and regulatory adherence.

Central to achieving reliable knowledge grounding is the development of comprehensive, structured metadata. Metadata acts as a detailed index or catalog that defines the meaning, context, and relationships of the underlying data, enabling AI to efficiently retrieve precise and meaningful insights. Without robust metadata, especially metadata structured in an AI-readable format grounding of knowledge cannot be successfully executed, resulting in unreliable answers, inaccuracies, and potential confusion or misdirection (often termed "AI hallucinations").

Below is an organized explanation of metadata creation for each knowledge source, highlighting the importance of AI-readable metadata:

1. Metadata for Structured Data:

Structured data resides primarily in databases, warehouses, or data lakes, clearly categorized with standardized schema.

- **Entities:**
  - Clearly defined human entities (patients, medical professionals at RWJ, bank customers, compliance officers).
  - Non-human entities (hospitals, clinics, pharmaceutical products, medical devices, bank accounts, investment instruments).
- **Entity Relations:**
  - Hierarchies clearly captured, such as corporate parent RWJ and its subsidiary hospitals and clinics.
  - Relationships explicitly defined patient-provider (RWJ), payer-hospital (RWJ), manufacturer-RWJ, client-account (United Bank).
- **Location:**
  - Geographical metadata clearly tagging location specifics (RWJ hospital locations, manufacturing sites, regional bank branches).
  - Essential for regional compliance and financial reporting, ensuring geographically accurate insights.
- **Transactions:**
  - Precisely categorized activities such as patient treatments, drug purchases, payments, rebates, contracts (RWJ and Manufacturers), banking transactions, loans, investments (United Bank).
- **Dates:**
  - Metadata clearly labeling transaction and event timelines (contract effective dates, treatment episodes, reimbursement periods, maturity dates for investments).
- **Metrics:**
  - Numeric indicators such as total revenue, patient count, treatment costs (RWJ), drug rebate percentages, ROI, profitability, QoQ growth rates (United Bank), clearly identified and consistently calculated.

2. Metadata for Documents:

Document repositories contain unstructured narratives, contracts, research papers, and regulatory documents, making metadata even more crucial for accurate interpretation.

- **Entities:**
  - Clearly annotated references to entities (RWJ clinics, Pharma/Biotech manufacturers, regulatory bodies like FDA or EMA, banking clients, investment partners).
- **Entity Relations:**
  - Document metadata highlighting references and context of relationships (contractual relationships between RWJ and pharma manufacturers, investor-client interactions at United Bank, legal agreements between entities).
- **Location:**
  - Clearly identifying location references in documents, crucial for understanding regulatory jurisdiction or market relevance (countries of operation, clinical trial locations, geographic regulatory differences).
- **Transactions:**
  - Metadata clearly defining document type (sales contracts, clinical trial agreements, banking loan agreements, compliance audits, regulatory filings).
- **Dates:**
  - Metadata explicitly capturing critical dates from documents (contract effective and expiration dates, policy release dates, regulatory compliance deadlines, audit periods).
- **Metrics:**
  - Document-level metadata outlining relevant numerical data (contract values, treatment efficacy metrics from research, credit risk assessments, loan amounts).

3. Metadata for News Feeds:

News feeds present dynamic, real-time data, requiring rapid extraction and contextual categorization through precise metadata.

- **Entities:**
  - Real-time identification of relevant entities such as RWJ, drug/device manufacturers, regulators, financial markets, banks, economic authorities.
- **Entity Relations:**
  - Metadata immediately capturing references of dynamic interactions (regulatory updates impacting RWJ compliance, mergers affecting United Bank, recalls announced by pharma/device manufacturers).
- **Location:**
  - Clearly tagging geographic regions referenced in news articles, enabling real-time tracking of regulatory developments or market impacts globally.
- **Transactions:**
  - Categorizing news types and activities clearly (market announcements, product recalls, regulatory updates, economic forecasts, banking policy changes).
- **Dates:**
  - Time-stamping events in news feeds precisely, enabling immediate integration into decision-making processes and scenario planning.
- **Metrics:**
  - Metadata tagging immediate numeric implications such as announced economic indicators (GDP forecasts, unemployment rates, currency fluctuations), new tariffs, market share impacts due to recalls or regulatory actions.

Why AI-Readable Metadata is Critical:

Building robust, AI-readable metadata is the most critical aspect of grounding knowledge, directly influencing the accuracy, relevance, and trustworthiness of the AI interface:

- **Contextual Clarity:**
  - Metadata provides AI with the necessary contextual clarity, allowing precise identification of relevant information and minimizing misunderstandings or misinterpretations.
- **Semantic Consistency:**
  - Ensures consistency across data sources, enabling AI to merge insights seamlessly from structured data, documents, and news feeds.
- **Efficient Retrieval:**
  - Enhances AI's capability to quickly navigate vast information repositories, dramatically improving response speed and accuracy.
- **Reduced Ambiguity:**
  - Clearly defined metadata significantly reduces ambiguity and enhances the reliability of responses provided to end-users.

Without effectively constructed and maintained metadata, grounding knowledge becomes virtually impossible. Metadata deficiencies directly compromise AI's ability to accurately retrieve and interpret information, leading to inaccuracies, inconsistencies, and potentially severe business impacts. Thus, careful and deliberate investment in AI-readable metadata is not merely beneficial it is indispensable for creating trusted, high-performance NLP-based AI applications that genuinely enhance decision-making capabilities across RWJ, pharmaceutical/device manufacturers, and United Bank.

Now, we will illustrate how a cross-functional NLP-based AI interface can effectively manage complex business queries across real-world scenarios involving RWJ Healthcare, pharmaceutical and medical device manufacturers, and United Bank. Through a structured, systematic approach, each scenario presented will be processed in a clearly defined workflow.

For every example provided, we will first create a precise, structured AI prompt to clearly define the user's intent. Following this, we will thoroughly break down the necessary information into the fundamental data types Entities, Entity Relations, Location, Transactions, Dates, and Metrics. For each data type, we will carefully specify the best data retrieval methods and logic, detailing how and from where data should be sourced. Lastly, we will define the ideal format and structure for the AI's response, ensuring that the outcomes strictly adhere to the critical standards of Reliability, Accuracy, and Trustworthiness.

This methodical approach is crucial, as it demonstrates how meticulous grounding of knowledge and thoughtfully engineered metadata facilitate precise and meaningful responses, significantly enhancing trust and efficiency across various business functions.

Event 1:

Fast Legs Corporation, a New Jersey-based medical device manufacturer specializing in implants such as hips and knees, is preparing its upcoming 10-K financial report. The CEO needs a detailed analysis of contract performance with its top ten customers, specifically highlighting Robert Wood Johnson (RWJ) Healthcare. RWJ contracts are executed at a corporate parent level, and the CEO specifically requests visibility into RWJ's business divided into 340B (hospitals qualifying for special federal discounts) and non-340B segments. Fast Legs' Master Data Management (MDM) system stores corporate parent identifiers, hospital locations, and their associated 340B statuses. Transaction-level shipment data units sold, invoice amounts, discounts, net sales, and prices reside in the data warehouse, while financial transactions at the corporate parent level reside in SAP. To confirm legitimate 340B transactions, shipment data must be validated daily against the Health Resources and Services Administration (HRSA) database, via API integration, ensuring transaction dates fall within authorized Covered Entity (CE) dates. Due to urgent board requirements, the CEO requests a concise, single-slide summary including five major contract terms (from a PDF), a table showing six rolling quarters of sales, net price, and quarter-over-quarter (QoQ) sales growth, and a comparative breakdown of the percentage of 340B versus non-340B business for RWJ relative to other top accounts, summarized in one sentence.

Metadata Required for Grounding Knowledge:

To manage this event efficiently, the following metadata elements must be created clearly in AI-readable format:

Entities:

RWJ (Corporate Parent, hospitals, clinics, 340B-designated entities)

Fast Legs Corporation

Other Top 10 Customer Organizations

HRSA (Government Entity)

CEO, Assistant

Entity Relations:

RWJ Corporate Parent ↔ RWJ Hospitals/Clinics (parent-child)

RWJ ↔ Fast Legs (Buyer–Supplier contract relationship)

RWJ 340B Locations ↔ HRSA (Regulatory compliance relation)

Location:

Hospital and clinic locations clearly identified as either 340B or non-340B

Headquarters locations (Fast Legs, RWJ)

Transactions:

Shipments (units, net sales, invoice amount, discounts)

Validated 340B transactions (HRSA database matching via API)

Contractual financial transactions recorded in SAP

Dates:

Shipment transaction dates

Contract effective and expiration dates

HRSA Covered Entity start/end dates

Rolling quarters clearly defined (six-quarter periods)

Metrics:

Net sales, net prices, discounts

QoQ Sales Growth (percentage)

Percentage split: 340B vs. non-340B business

Traditional (non-AI) Workflow for Assistant:

Without AI, the assistant would perform the following detailed steps manually:

Extract Contract Terms:

Locate the specific contract PDF from the document repository.

Manually read and summarize the top 5 contract terms.

SQL Queries for Shipment Data:

Join shipment transactions table (Data Warehouse) to MDM to identify RWJ's corporate parent ID and related hospitals.

Write and run SQL to pull transaction data (units, net sales, invoice amounts, discounts, net price) by RWJ locations.

Categorize transactions into 340B/non-340B using location types and transaction types.

Validation via HRSA Database:

Create an additional SQL query/API call to HRSA DB to confirm CE Start and End dates.

Validate each transaction's date against the HRSA dataset.

Ensure only valid 340B transactions are flagged as 340B.

Quarterly Data Aggregation:

Write additional SQL aggregations to compute net sales, net prices for six rolling quarters.

Calculate QoQ sales growth manually in Excel or SQL.

Comparative Analysis:

Aggregate RWJ 340B vs. non-340B percentages.

Perform similar aggregations for other top accounts.

Generate one-sentence summary manually.

Presentation Slide Preparation:

Manually create a PowerPoint slide, entering summarized contract terms, tables, and analysis.

AI-Powered Workflow:

AI Prompt:

"Prepare a single-slide summary for RWJ Healthcare's contract performance for the past six quarters. Extract the top five summarized contract terms from the RWJ contract PDF. Generate a table displaying six rolling quarters of Sales, Net Price, and QoQ Sales Growth. Validate and categorize transactions as 340B or non-340B by cross-referencing HRSA database dates. Also, include a comparative one-sentence summary of RWJ's 340B versus non-340B percentage against other top 10 customer accounts. Ensure output accuracy, reliability, and trustworthiness."

AI Breakdown of Data Types from the Prompt:

Entities: RWJ Healthcare, Fast Legs Corporation, HRSA, Other Top 10 Customers.

Entity Relations: Contracts (RWJ–Fast Legs), Regulatory validation (RWJ–HRSA).

Location: Hospitals (340B/non-340B), RWJ Corporate Parent.

Transactions: Shipment records (units, price, discounts, net sales), Contract Financial records (SAP).

Dates: Transaction dates, rolling quarterly periods, HRSA start/end dates.

Metrics: Net sales, net price, QoQ growth, % 340B vs. non-340B business.

Data Sources & Extraction Logic (AI-driven):

Structured Data:

Source: Data Warehouse (shipment transactions), SAP (financial data), MDM (parent/location IDs).

Logic:

Join shipment table and MDM to classify locations as 340B or non-340B.

Run SQL/API integrations automatically against HRSA DB daily to validate 340B dates.

Aggregate quarterly data, auto-calculate net sales, net price, QoQ growth.

Documents:

Source: Contract PDF in document repository.

Logic:

NLP extraction logic: Summarize key contractual terms (discount rates, payment terms, rebates, performance terms).

Use semantic understanding models trained specifically on legal/financial language.

News Feeds:

Not required for this specific request.

Structured AI Output (Slide Format for Immediate Copy-Paste):

Contract Summary (5 key terms):

- Pricing and Discount Terms: 340B pricing validated quarterly via HRSA, commercial discounts structured in 4 tiers ranging from 5% to 15% based on annual purchase volume.
- Payment Terms and Conditions: Invoices payable Net 60 days; 2% discount if paid within 30 days; late payments incur 1.5% monthly interest.
- Performance and Delivery Obligations: Guaranteed product shipment within 10 business days; 98% minimum accuracy and fulfillment compliance required.
- Contract Duration and Renewal: Three-year initial term, automatic annual renewal thereafter unless terminated with 60-day notice.
- Regulatory and Compliance Requirements: Compliance with FDA guidelines mandatory; quarterly validation of 340B eligibility via HRSA database required.

Six Rolling Quarters Analysis:

Quarter	Net Sales ($)	Net Price ($)	QoQ Sales Growth (%)
Q1'23	2,500,000	1,000	-
Q2'23	2,650,000	1,010	6.0%
Q3'23	2,800,000	1,015	5.7%
Q4'23	2,950,000	1,020	5.4%
Q1'24	3,100,000	1,030	5.1%
Q2'24	3,200,000	1,035	3.2%

Comparative Summary (One sentence):

RWJ's 340B business accounts for 42% of total sales, slightly above the average (38%) among top ten customers.

Validation (Ensuring Reliability, Accuracy, Trust):

- AI provides validation markers:
- HRSA validation (dates matched, API status).
- Source DB timestamps for data extraction.

- Confidence scores for PDF extraction accuracy.
- SQL/API logs accessible for audits.

The assistant receives the clearly structured, verified slide format, ready to directly copy-paste into the CEO's PowerPoint presentation.

The assistant extracts the SQL statements automatically generated by the AI interface from system logs, carefully reviews and confirms that the SQL logic employs accurate identifiers, correct joins, and adheres strictly to business rules particularly ensuring accurate joins between the shipment table, corporate parent records from MDM, and HRSA validation via API. The assistant then independently executes these validated SQL queries against the data warehouse, SAP financial data, and HRSA database to cross-check and validate the accuracy and consistency of the NLP interface output. The assistant verifies numerical figures, such as quarterly sales, net prices, and 340B versus non-340B transaction splits, precisely match between the AI-generated output and manual SQL execution results. Additionally, the assistant performs a cursory 'find' search within the original contract PDF to confirm that the extracted contract terms presented by the AI tool align accurately with the actual contract language. This structured validation ensures the assistant can confidently trust the accuracy and reliability of the AI-generated content, significantly reducing the potential for inaccuracies and errors in the critical report being prepared for the CEO.

Had the assistant completed this task without an NLP-based AI interface, it would typically require approximately 6-8 hours to manually write complex SQL queries, independently cross-reference HRSA compliance via separate API integrations, manually extract and summarize contract terms from the PDF, and prepare accurate calculations of QoQ growth and comparative analysis. However, leveraging the NLP-driven AI interface, including validation and cross-verification, reduced the total time required to roughly 30-45 minutes, substantially improving efficiency and allowing the assistant to focus on validation and high-level analytical checks rather than labor-intensive manual data processing.

The substantial efficiency gain was made possible primarily through the comprehensive grounding of knowledge with structured, AI-readable metadata. Metadata ensured accurate identification, contextual clarity, and seamless integration across structured data, documents, and external regulatory data sources such as HRSA. Without meticulously structured metadata, the AI interface would have struggled to locate and interpret relevant data points effectively, leading to incorrect or ambiguous query results, significant manual correction efforts, potential compliance risks, inaccuracies in financial reporting, and a subsequent erosion of trust in the AI-generated insights. Thus, well-structured metadata was critically essential, not only facilitating rapid data retrieval but also guaranteeing reliable, precise, and contextually accurate outcomes.

Event 2:

Bioncology, an oncology-focused pharmaceutical company, is conducting Phase 3 clinical trials for two promising drugs intended to treat metastasized cancers. The company enlisted a prominent oncologist from RWJ Healthcare as both Principal Investigator (PI) and key researcher for these critical trials. Known widely as a Key Opinion Leader (KOL), this oncologist was recognized for clinical research excellence and served as a PI for multiple pharmaceutical companies. In January 2025, the CEO of Bioncology received troubling information via a news article reporting that an oncology startup had uncovered evidence indicating that this same PI deliberately altered clinical trial data, skewing test results to present a falsely favorable outcome. Given the PI's involvement in Bioncology's trials, the CEO urgently tasked the Chief of Staff to identify the necessary compliance and remedial actions to address the issue proactively, ensure regulatory compliance, and mitigate potential reputational and operational damage to the company.

Using the NLP-driven AI Interface:

AI Prompt:

"An RWJ-based Principal Investigator for Bioncology's Phase 3 oncology trials has been implicated in deliberate clinical trial data falsification by another pharmaceutical company. Immediately identify and list all regulatory compliance and mitigation actions Bioncology must undertake to manage this critical event effectively and minimize legal, reputational, and operational risks."

AI Breakdown of Data Types from Prompt:

- **Entities:** Bioncology, RWJ-based PI/Oncologist, Oncology Startup, FDA, EMA, Regulatory Agencies.
- **Entity Relations:** PI relationship to Bioncology, PI-KOL status for multiple pharma companies, RWJ affiliation.
- **Location:** RWJ facilities conducting trials, trial locations identified in Phase 3 trial documentation.
- **Transactions:** Clinical trial data submissions, contractual engagements with PI, regulatory filings.
- **Dates:** Clinical trial periods, news article date (January 2025), timelines for regulatory reporting.
- **Metrics:** Clinical trial outcomes and statistical significance data previously reported.

Data Sources & Extraction Logic (AI-driven):

- **Structured Data:**
    - Clinical trial management systems, investigator compliance databases, clinical trial registries (CT.gov, FDA/EMA submissions).
    - Logic: Query all structured data for trials associated with the implicated PI; match data submission timelines, outcomes, and compliance documentation.
- **Documents:**
    - Clinical trial protocols, informed consent forms, signed Investigator agreements/contracts.
    - Logic: Extract key obligations, compliance requirements, misconduct clauses, reporting mandates, and corrective action terms from contracts and regulatory documents.
- **News Feeds:**

    - Real-time extraction of news reporting details, reputational risks, and regulatory responses from relevant authorities.
    - Logic: Capture immediate insights from news sources, public statements from regulators, and historical similar cases for precedence.

AI-generated List of Actions (Intelligently Identified):

- Immediately suspend the implicated PI from ongoing clinical trials and document formal notification.
- Conduct an internal audit of clinical data associated with the implicated PI across all trial sites.
- Notify FDA, EMA, and other relevant regulatory agencies immediately, as per regulatory compliance guidelines.
- Retain external legal counsel specializing in regulatory compliance and clinical trial integrity issues.
- Inform RWJ corporate management officially regarding the ongoing situation and actions taken.
- Issue a public statement outlining steps being taken to maintain transparency and integrity.
- Assemble a crisis response team internally to manage stakeholder communications and regulatory interactions.
- Secure external independent reviewers to re-validate existing clinical data from trials involving the PI.
- Establish a compliance timeline and comprehensive corrective action plan to rectify data integrity issues.
- Review and reinforce internal compliance training programs for all investigators and research staff.

Chief of Staff Workflow without NLP-driven AI (Traditional Approach):

Without NLP assistance, the Chief of Staff would perform extensive manual efforts:

1. Personally read and analyze the news article, documenting specific allegations.
2. Immediately contact legal and compliance teams for regulatory guidance.
3. Request an emergency internal meeting with clinical operations and data management teams.
4. Manually identify all clinical trial contracts involving the implicated PI, reviewing investigator obligations, compliance clauses, and misconduct protocols.
5. Independently search FDA, EMA, and regulatory agency websites for compliance guidelines and mandatory reporting timelines regarding investigator misconduct.
6. Schedule emergency calls with external regulatory experts and legal counsel to confirm obligations.
7. Conduct manual internal data audits, which would involve significant resources from the clinical research, regulatory, compliance, and data-management teams.
8. Prepare a compliance and risk mitigation report for immediate presentation to the CEO and board.

This manual approach would typically require 2-3 days of intensive multi-departmental collaboration, presenting substantial risk of oversight and delay.

Validation Methodology with NLP-driven AI Interface:

The Chief of Staff validates AI-generated actions by performing the following steps:

- Extract and review SQL/API logs from NLP system to ensure all relevant regulatory databases, contracts, and trial data were accurately identified and queried.
- Cross-reference AI-generated compliance actions against official FDA, EMA, and ICH-GCP guidelines to

verify comprehensiveness and accuracy.
- Perform a manual check of key terms in investigator contracts to ensure AI's extracted recommendations align precisely with existing contractual obligations.
- Independently validate AI-recommended actions with internal legal and compliance teams for confirmation and completeness.

By utilizing the NLP-based AI interface, the Chief of Staff's total time spent including validations is reduced dramatically to approximately 1-2 hours, compared to several days of manual effort.

Metadata Definitions Required to Generate the Compliance Action List:

Entities:

Clearly defined labels for Human entities (Principal Investigator, CEO, Chief of Staff, Regulatory Officers, Clinical Research Personnel) and Non-human entities (Bioncology, RWJ, FDA, EMA, Oncology Startup, Clinical Research Organizations, Legal Advisors).

Entity Relations:

Explicit metadata indicating contractual and legal relationships (Bioncology–PI contractual relationship, PI–RWJ affiliation, Bioecology–Regulatory Agencies (FDA/EMA), Bioncology–Clinical Research Organizations, Bioncology–Legal Advisors).

Location:

Structured geographical identifiers for Clinical Trial Sites, Regulatory Jurisdictions (FDA-US, EMA-EU), RWJ Hospital locations, and PI's associated research facilities.

Transactions:

Metadata clearly categorizing Clinical Trial activities (data collection, data submission, protocol adherence), Regulatory Compliance filings, Contract execution, Investigator payments, Internal Audit procedures, and Public disclosures.

Dates:

Explicit metadata definitions for Clinical Trial periods (trial initiation, completion dates, data submission deadlines), Regulatory reporting timelines (notification deadlines upon discovering misconduct), Contractual obligation timelines (contract start, termination, misconduct reporting requirements), Internal Audit schedules, and Crisis Response milestones.

Metrics:

Clear numeric definitions and categorizations for Clinical Trial performance metrics (patient enrollment numbers, reported outcomes, adherence rates), Regulatory compliance metrics (timelines, notifications made), and Risk management metrics (identified risks, mitigation completion rates).

These comprehensive metadata definitions enable precise identification, swift retrieval, and accurate correlation of all required information, empowering an NLP-driven AI interface to reliably generate a complete and accurate set of compliance and remedial actions.

Importance of Metadata in Grounding Knowledge:

This dramatic efficiency improvement was possible only due to structured, AI-readable metadata grounding, enabling the NLP system to rapidly identify, retrieve, and correlate relevant regulatory data, clinical trial records, investigator contracts, and historical compliance cases. Without meticulously structured metadata, the AI interface would fail to accurately link critical compliance actions with relevant data points and regulatory obligations, leading to partial or incorrect recommendations. Poor or missing metadata would force the Chief of Staff back to manual processes, significantly increasing the risk of regulatory penalties, reputational damage, delayed crisis management, and potentially severe operational disruptions. Therefore, the comprehensive grounding of knowledge using clearly defined metadata proved indispensable in effectively responding to this critical compliance and reputational event.

Event 3:

In response to tariffs introduced by the U.S. administration effective from Q2 2025, several countries within the European Union (EU), along with the UK and non-EU European nations, are reportedly considering substantial interest rate cuts ranging from 50 to 150 basis points to stimulate their local economies and counterbalance reduced exports. United Bank, holding significant market share in personal and corporate banking sectors across these regions, faces strategic impacts from such monetary policy changes. Although no official announcements have been made by central banks yet, multiple reputable financial analysts and news outlets are reporting on the likelihood of these interest rate reductions. To swiftly respond, the CEO of United Bank has tasked the Chief Economist with validating these claims, assessing their accuracy, estimating total potential interest rate cuts, and identifying the expected timing and intervals. The Chief Economist must summarize the analysis clearly into a single slide to support board-level decision-making regarding resource allocation to effectively manage the impending rate adjustments.

Using the NLP-driven AI Interface:

AI Prompt:

"Gather all recent analyst reports, economic forecasts, and news articles from credible financial news outlets regarding anticipated interest rate cuts (50-150 basis points) in EU, UK, and non-EU European countries due to new U.S. tariffs starting Q2 2025. Extract predictions on total rate reductions, timing, and intervals for these cuts. Summarize clearly in one slide for CEO review."

AI Breakdown of Data Types from Prompt:

- **Entities:** United Bank, European Central Bank (ECB), Bank of England (BoE), central banks of non-EU European countries, financial analysts, news outlets, regulatory and governmental authorities.
- **Entity Relations:** United Bank–Central Banks, Central Banks–Analysts, Analysts–News Outlets.
- **Location:** EU member states, United Kingdom, and other impacted European countries.
- **Transactions:** Monetary policy decisions, tariff announcements, analyst economic forecasts, central bank announcements.
- **Dates:** Tariff implementation date (Q2 2025), anticipated timelines for rate reductions, interval dates for potential rate cuts.
- **Metrics:** Interest rate changes in basis points, cumulative rate reductions, market response projections, economic growth impact metrics.

Data Sources & Extraction Logic (AI-driven):

Structured Data:

- *Source:* Economic databases (central bank historical rate adjustments, GDP forecasts, market impact analysis databases).

Logic:

- Automatically query historical structured data related to interest rate responses to previous tariff impositions.

- Retrieve historical central bank rate adjustments, comparing past forecasts to actual outcomes.

Documents:

- *Source:* Analyst economic forecast reports, internal market analysis memos, regulatory and central bank policy review documents.

Logic:

- NLP extraction of predicted rate adjustments, timelines, and intervals detailed in analyst and central bank forecast documents.
- Identify and extract forecasts and economic reasoning from official and semi-official reports.

News Feeds:

- *Source:* Bloomberg, Reuters, Financial Times, and central banks' official news feeds.

Logic:

- Semantic and sentiment analysis to gauge analyst consensus on anticipated rate cuts.
- Aggregate recent news insights into predicted timing, intervals, and scope of anticipated monetary policy changes.

Chief Economist Workflow without NLP-driven AI (Traditional Approach):

Without NLP-driven AI assistance, the Chief Economist would:

1. Manually review recent news and analyst reports from reputable sources (Bloomberg, Financial Times, Reuters).
2. Personally verify central bank official statements or hints through ECB, Bank of England, and central bank websites.
3. Assemble an economic analysis team to manually gather historical interest rate responses to tariffs, market impacts, and economic outcomes.
4. Manually analyze historical monetary policy documents and past analyst forecasts to contextualize current predictions.
5. Perform manual statistical analysis to estimate the timing and intervals of interest rate cuts based on historical precedents and recent market signals.
6. Create a detailed but concise summary in a presentation slide format, manually preparing the charts and summaries required.

This traditional approach would likely require approximately 1–2 full days involving intensive collaboration with economic analysis teams and would involve substantial manual effort, risk of oversight, and potential delays.

Validation by the Chief Economist (Ensuring Reliability, Accuracy, Trust):

The AI-driven NLP interface significantly streamlines data gathering, automatically consolidating extensive structured economic data, analyst forecasts, and news analysis rapidly. However, due to the nuanced emotional, situational, and political contexts underlying monetary policy decisions which AI inherently lacks the Chief Economist must personally validate and contextualize this data. Specifically, the Chief Economist will:

- Review original analyst reports and central bank documents cited by AI to confirm data accuracy and interpretative context.
- Independently assess economic reasoning presented by analysts to ensure political feasibility, historical alignment, and consistency with macroeconomic trends.
- Cross-verify AI-extracted forecast timelines, intervals, and projected basis-point reductions with reputable central bank statements or credible news sources.
- Perform a critical review of the AI-generated slide to confirm clarity, conciseness, and appropriateness for board-level communication.

Metadata Definitions Required for Economic and Financial Events:

Entities:

Clearly defined identifiers for human entities (Chief Economist, CEO, Financial Analysts, Regulators, Central Bank Officials) and non-human entities (United Bank, Central Banks such as ECB and Bank of England, Financial Markets, Tariffs, Governmental Bodies).

Entity Relations:

Metadata explicitly categorizing relationships such as regulatory oversight (United Bank–Central Banks), analyst reporting relationships (Financial Analysts–Financial News Sources), economic dependency relationships (Central Banks–National Economies, Interest Rates–Market Demand), and governmental interactions (Regulatory Authorities–Banks).

Location:

Explicit geographic metadata definitions including operational regions (EU countries, UK, non-EU European nations), jurisdictional locations of regulatory bodies, and market-specific locations impacted by economic policy changes.

Transactions:

Detailed classification of transactions, including monetary policy announcements, tariff implementation notifications, central bank rate adjustments, economic forecasts from analysts, strategic resource allocation decisions, and corporate planning responses.

Dates:

Clearly defined and structured date metadata including tariff implementation dates, central bank policy announcement dates, projected rate cut periods, economic forecast issuance dates, validation timeline for analyst predictions, and planned strategic response timelines.

Metrics:

Comprehensive numeric metric definitions such as interest rate changes (basis points), total cumulative rate reductions, GDP growth forecasts, consumer and corporate demand forecasts, currency exchange rate variations, and strategic impact measures (resource allocation metrics, risk assessment scores, and market-share analysis).

This structured metadata set is essential for reliably and efficiently grounding economic and financial knowledge, enabling accurate, trustworthy, and timely AI-supported decision-making. This metadata framework will consistently apply across all future economic and financial events and scenarios.

Efficiency Gains and Importance of Metadata:

Leveraging the NLP-driven AI interface reduces total analysis and validation time significantly from 1–2 days to approximately 1–2 hours. The extensive, structured metadata underpinning this knowledge grounding plays a crucial role, enabling AI systems to swiftly identify, accurately retrieve, and clearly summarize vast quantities of structured economic data, news reports, and analytical documentation. Without carefully curated and structured metadata, the AI system could neither rapidly nor reliably gather the necessary data for the Chief Economist's validation. Missing or insufficient metadata would compel the Chief Economist to revert entirely to manual data collection, significantly increasing analysis timelines, potentially missing critical policy windows, misaligning resource allocation, and increasing the risk of strategic errors. Thus, structured, AI-readable metadata is indispensable for timely, accurate, and trustworthy economic analyses that inform strategic decisions in a rapidly evolving policy environment.

Event 4:

United Bank, a leading player in India's auto loan sector, recently discovered a significant fraud operation involving a network of loan-processing agents across three Indian states. These agents deceitfully modified customer loan applications to include themselves as co-owners of vehicles financed by unsuspecting individuals, subsequently securing additional unauthorized loans against those same vehicles. The Government of India has responded by issuing a show-cause notice, demanding that United Bank submit a comprehensive report detailing the full scope of financial losses, identification of perpetrators, legal actions initiated, and adherence to regulatory requirements within 90 days. Non-compliance could lead to severe repercussions, including potential suspension of the bank's operational license in India. Consequently, the Country Manager urgently needs to assemble an expert crisis-response team, engage top-tier external legal advisors, public relations firms, and financial forensic investigators, and also secure a detailed breakdown of applicable government regulatory policies governing such fraud events.

Using the NLP-driven AI Interface:

AI Prompt:

"Identify the full scope and impact of the recently discovered auto-loan fraud involving agents in three Indian states. Extract data on affected accounts, total financial impact, compliance requirements, and recommended legal actions based on current regulatory guidelines from the Government of India and RBI. Additionally, recommend highly reputable external legal firms, forensic auditors, and PR agencies specialized in financial fraud response. Summarize clearly into a structured report outline for immediate regulatory submission."

AI Breakdown of Data Types from Prompt:

- **Entities:** United Bank, Customers, Auto-loan Agents, Government of India, Reserve Bank of India (RBI), External Legal Firms, Forensic Auditors, PR Agencies.
- **Entity Relations:** Relationships between United Bank and its agents, loan agent-customer interactions, regulatory relationships (United Bank–RBI/Government), external advisory relationships (United Bank–Legal/PR/Forensics).
- **Location:** Indian states impacted by fraud, United Bank's regional presence, regulatory jurisdiction (India-level, state-level).
- **Transactions:** Fraudulent loan activities, secondary loan applications, account modifications, regulatory reporting, compliance actions.
- **Dates:** Loan origination dates, fraud detection dates, government notice issuance date, mandated 90-day reporting deadline.
- **Metrics:** Financial amounts defrauded, total fraudulent loans identified, number of affected customers, potential penalties.

Data Sources & Extraction Logic (AI-driven):

Structured Data:

- **Source:** Loan Management Systems, Customer Database, Agent-Attribution Databases, Financial Accounting Systems.

Logic:

- Identify accounts associated with implicated agents by querying application modification logs and timestamps.
- Automatically flag anomalies indicating unauthorized application changes or duplicate loans.
- Aggregate total financial impact from fraudulent loans identified.

Documents:

- *Source:* Regulatory compliance manuals, legal policies, agent contracts, historical fraud investigation reports, RBI compliance documents.

Logic:

- Extract compliance steps, legal obligations, mandated timelines, and reporting requirements clearly defined in regulatory and internal policy documents.
- Identify recommended fraud management procedures from previous internal documents or RBI guidelines.

News Feeds:

- *Source:* Regulatory announcements, Government of India and RBI press statements, Financial news agencies (Economic Times, Business Standard).

Logic:

- Rapid extraction of recent announcements and policy responses, particularly RBI statements and regulatory frameworks related to fraud management.

Workflow without NLP-driven AI (Traditional Approach):

Without NLP-driven AI support, the Country Manager and response team would:

1. Initiate a manual audit, reviewing loan applications and account records individually to uncover fraudulent entries attributed to implicated agents.
2. Manually identify patterns across application modifications, involving significant internal forensic resources and prolonged investigation timelines.
3. Personally consult internal regulatory compliance documentation and government guidelines from RBI, manually identifying mandated actions and reporting requirements.
4. Individually contact and vet external legal advisors, financial forensic auditors, and PR firms to manage the incident response.
5. Assemble multiple internal teams for collaborative review of findings, compiling detailed documentation into a compliant regulatory report.
6. Manually validate findings through cross-functional meetings and external consultations.

Such a manual approach would likely require several weeks or longer, greatly increasing operational disruption, regulatory non-compliance risks, and potential reputational damage.

Validation by the Country Manager and Team (Ensuring Reliability, Accuracy, Trust):

Given the sensitive, nuanced, and situationally complex nature of financial fraud incidents, AI-generated data will primarily serve to accelerate initial information gathering and analysis. The Country Manager and internal experts must personally:

- Independently verify AI-identified fraudulent applications, cross-referencing loan application logs, timestamps, and agent attribution data.
- Review and validate recommended compliance steps extracted from RBI and government regulatory documents.
- Personally, vet external firms (legal, forensic, PR) identified by AI through direct interaction and reputation validation.
- Cross-check structured AI outputs against internal records and regulatory guidelines to ensure full accuracy, completeness, and relevance to the current scenario.

Efficiency Gains and Importance of Metadata:

By leveraging NLP-driven AI, United Bank dramatically accelerates the fraud investigation and compliance-response timeline, reducing the overall time required from several weeks to just a few days, significantly improving the bank's ability to comply with the mandated regulatory deadline. Robustly structured, AI-readable metadata is pivotal in enabling rapid, accurate extraction and correlation of loan application data, agent attribution details, regulatory obligations, and recommended actions. Without precise, structured metadata, the AI system would be incapable of swiftly and accurately identifying relevant application anomalies, fraudulent patterns, compliance requirements, or qualified external resources. Missing or poorly structured metadata would necessitate extensive manual validation efforts, severely prolonging investigation and reporting timelines, heightening the risk of missed deadlines, non-compliance penalties, and reputational damage. Thus, comprehensive metadata definitions become essential to efficiently manage high-stakes fraud scenarios.

Metadata Definitions Required for Financial Fraud and Compliance Events:

Entities:

Clearly identified and structured human entities (Loan Agents, Customers, Country Manager, Regulatory Officials, Legal Experts, PR Specialists, Financial Forensic Investigators) and non-human entities (United Bank, RBI, Government of India, External Consulting Firms).

Entity Relations:

Explicitly defined relationships including loan agent–customer associations (for attribution and identification of fraud), bank–agent contractual relations, bank–regulatory bodies for compliance, and external resource engagements (legal, PR, forensic investigators).

Location:

Explicit geographical identification metadata for Indian states involved in the fraud, regional and local operational presence, regulatory jurisdiction and oversight.

Transactions:

Detailed classification metadata capturing loan applications, fraudulent modifications, loan approvals, second loan disbursements, regulatory compliance filings, and fraud response activities.

Dates:

Clearly structured metadata including dates of loan originations, fraudulent alterations, discovery timelines, government-issued notice dates, regulatory reporting deadlines, and legal-action timelines.

Metrics:

Clearly defined numeric metrics metadata covering the financial amount impacted, number of fraudulent loans identified, total customers affected, regulatory penalties anticipated, compliance milestones achieved, and investigation progress metrics.

This comprehensive, structured metadata framework ensures rapid, accurate, and reliable grounding of knowledge, essential for swiftly responding to critical financial fraud and compliance events at United Bank.

The prompts for the four detailed scenarios explored above spanning healthcare compliance, pharmaceutical regulatory management, international monetary policy response, and financial fraud investigation may appear ambitious and expansive. However, they are practically achievable when approached with a robust, structured methodology. As demonstrated, grounding knowledge through meticulous data engineering is foundational but represents only one essential component in building effective AI-driven systems. To fully operationalize such expansive prompts, two additional foundational pillars AI Agents and Human Digital Twins are equally critical. AI Agents efficiently execute complex tasks, rapidly extracting and synthesizing data, while Human Digital Twins replicate sophisticated human cognitive processes, interpreting context, and orchestrating meaningful responses. In the upcoming chapters, we will delve deeply into these two remaining pillars, illustrating how their integration with data engineering completes the framework necessary for realizing the full potential of powerful, real-world AI applications.

To effectively join and integrate the three diverse knowledge stores structured data, documents, and news feeds into a cohesive, reliable source of knowledge, a specialized technique known as Named Entity Recognition (NER) is particularly beneficial. NER is an advanced natural language processing method that identifies and classifies key pieces of information from unstructured textual data. Here, the term "entity" does not refer to the data-engineering categories discussed earlier, but rather denotes real-world objects or concepts, such as people's names, organizational titles, geographic locations, dates, or financial figures. For instance, in a news article discussing regulatory actions by the Reserve Bank of India, NER would accurately detect "Reserve Bank of India" as an organization, "India" as a location, and dates related to policy announcements.

Named Entity Recognition is critical because it enables AI systems to extract structured and actionable information from extensive unstructured textual documents, contracts, regulatory guidelines, or real-time news articles. By clearly identifying and categorizing these real-world entities, AI systems can seamlessly relate information across all three knowledge stores. For example, NER can automatically recognize references to regulatory agencies in both structured databases (as standard identifiers), documents (regulatory guidelines), and news feeds (recent policy announcements), thus significantly simplifying the process of integrating and synthesizing relevant knowledge.

However, despite NER's powerful capabilities, it may not always perfectly manage certain complexities inherent in text data. Challenges may include ambiguous references, context-sensitive interpretations, or subtle linguistic nuances. When NER proves insufficient, alternative methods such as Topic Modeling and Semantic Analysis may be employed. Topic Modeling, which identifies themes and concepts across extensive textual collections, can broadly categorize content even without explicit named entities. Similarly, Semantic Analysis techniques, such as sentiment analysis or semantic role labeling, interpret the deeper meanings, contexts, and relationships within text, providing valuable insights when straightforward named entities are ambiguous or absent.

In situations where NER alone is inadequate, leveraging these alternative techniques ensures robust integration across structured data, document repositories, and dynamic news feeds. For instance, if a regulatory document uses generalized language without explicitly naming entities, topic modeling can identify thematic areas such as "financial compliance," "data privacy," or "loan fraud" thus enabling the system to classify and integrate relevant content effectively. Similarly, semantic analysis can help discern subtle differences in sentiment or context that influence decision-making, especially when interpreting nuanced financial analyst reports or policy statements.

Thus, while Named Entity Recognition remains the cornerstone method for linking diverse information sources within an AI-driven knowledge framework, the inclusion of complementary methods like Topic Modeling and Semantic Analysis ensures comprehensive and accurate knowledge integration. This combination enables a robust understanding of context, maintains clarity, enhances accuracy, and substantially increases the reliability of AI-generated insights ensuring that expansive and ambitious prompts are not only achievable but reliably actionable in real-world decision-making contexts.

A detailed exploration of Named Entity Recognition (NER), along with alternative text-analysis techniques such as Topic Modeling, Semantic Analysis, and other advanced natural language processing methods, will be comprehensively covered in a dedicated companion volume focused exclusively on Data Engineering, also known as Grounding Knowledge. This forthcoming book will provide readers with extensive real-world examples, detailed case studies, and practical illustrations, clearly demonstrating how these sophisticated techniques can be applied effectively to various knowledge sources structured data, complex documents, and dynamic news feeds to enable powerful, context-aware AI solutions.

The pillar of Data Engineering, or Grounding Knowledge, is not merely beneficial but absolutely critical to successful AI application and adoption. Without a thoroughly grounded and carefully structured knowledge base, AI systems become vulnerable to inaccuracies, inconsistencies, and even severe misinterpretations known as hallucinations, which significantly erode trust. Effective data engineering provides AI systems with reliable, standardized, and context-rich information, ensuring accurate results and meaningful insights. By carefully grounding knowledge through structured, detailed metadata, organizations create a foundation that empowers AI solutions to deliver clarity, reliability, and actionable intelligence essential for high-stakes decision-making in complex real-world scenarios.

Moreover, Data Engineering does not operate in isolation; rather, it fundamentally enables the other two critical pillars AI Agents and Human Digital Twins to function effectively. AI Agents, designed to rapidly perform data-intensive and repetitive tasks, depend explicitly on clearly structured and meticulously engineered data to operate seamlessly and reliably. Human Digital Twins, which replicate complex human cognitive processes and nuanced contextual interpretations, similarly rely upon grounded, structured knowledge to accurately interpret scenarios and guide meaningful decision-making. Thus, without the robust, reliable foundation provided by comprehensive Data Engineering, the sophisticated capabilities of AI Agents and Human Digital Twins cannot be fully realized, making Grounding Knowledge not just important but indispensable to the practical success and widespread adoption of powerful, transformative AI applications.

AI Agents: Executing Complex Tasks and Driving Contextual Accuracy in AI Applications

Having established the foundational importance of Data Engineering also known as Grounding Knowledge we now move to the next critical pillar: AI Agents. While Grounding Knowledge organizes and standardizes vast repositories of structured data, documents, and real-time news feeds, it is AI Agents that operationally execute tasks and transform grounded data into practical outputs. AI Agents are specialized software components capable of rapidly performing defined tasks that traditionally require significant human effort, reducing manual workloads and enabling quicker, more precise responses across complex business scenarios such as those described in Events 1 through 4.

AI Agents can be broadly categorized into three distinct types: Data Agents, Domain Agents, and Utility Agents. Data Agents are responsible for efficiently retrieving, validating, and formatting data from structured databases, documents, or news feeds, directly supporting data accuracy in scenarios like Event 1 (RWJ contract analysis). Domain Agents possess specialized expertise in specific fields such as healthcare compliance (Event 2: Bioncology investigation) or financial analytics (Events 3 and 4: United Bank scenarios), applying targeted domain knowledge to accurately interpret complex requirements. Utility Agents facilitate routine operational tasks, including generating SQL queries, updating compliance records, and coordinating interactions between Data and Domain Agents, thereby ensuring smooth operational execution. Together, these three types of AI Agents comprehensively support robust AI solutions by converting grounded knowledge into actionable, context-specific outputs.

AI Agents represent a specialized category of software designed to execute defined tasks that typically require deliberate human effort. Unlike traditional software routines, an AI Agent interacts dynamically with structured and unstructured information sources, performing operations such as retrieving, validating, and formatting information according to clearly defined instructions. Rather than mimicking human reasoning or emotional context, AI Agents focus strictly on well-defined tasks, applying a consistent logic-based approach to complete repetitive or resource-intensive activities that might otherwise consume considerable human resources and time.

In contrast to Human Digital Twins, which serve as virtual counterparts to human roles and are designed to simulate human cognitive capabilities AI Agents maintain a purely task-oriented scope. While a Human Digital Twin attempts to replicate the complexity and nuances of human cognitive processing, including interpretation and contextual understanding, an AI Agent acts within a precise operational boundary. For instance, when tasked with examining financial documents, the agent precisely follows a defined process, extracting and organizing relevant information without interpreting the broader business implications or considering emotional factors that might influence human judgment.

An essential characteristic of AI Agents lies in their ability to perform consistently at high speeds, processing large volumes of data far more rapidly than human personnel. For example, within a financial investigation like Event 4 involving United Bank India's auto loan fraud, AI Agents would swiftly identify discrepancies by quickly parsing loan application records, account modifications, and associated agent identifiers. They execute these tasks rapidly and methodically, significantly reducing time to complete foundational investigative activities.

AI Agents operate strictly within the instructions they are provided, without independent deviation or judgment. They lack subjective reasoning or adaptability outside their prescribed scope, making them ideally suited for highly repetitive or standardized tasks where consistency and repeatability are crucial. Consequently, tasks requiring subjective judgment, situational adaptation, or emotional sensitivity remain firmly outside the operational scope of an AI Agent and continue to necessitate direct human oversight or Human Digital Twin intervention.

The philosophy underpinning AI Agents is one of purposeful precision and clarity. They function as reliable, consistent instruments explicitly crafted to execute operationally defined tasks, reducing human effort and significantly accelerating critical processes. By focusing solely on explicitly specified tasks, these agents become essential components within the broader AI framework, complementing both grounded knowledge provided by Data Engineering and the contextual understanding offered by Human Digital Twins. This clarity of purpose defines their role and ensures their effectiveness across diverse business environments such as healthcare, pharmaceuticals, banking, and financial analysis as illustrated in Events 1 through 4.

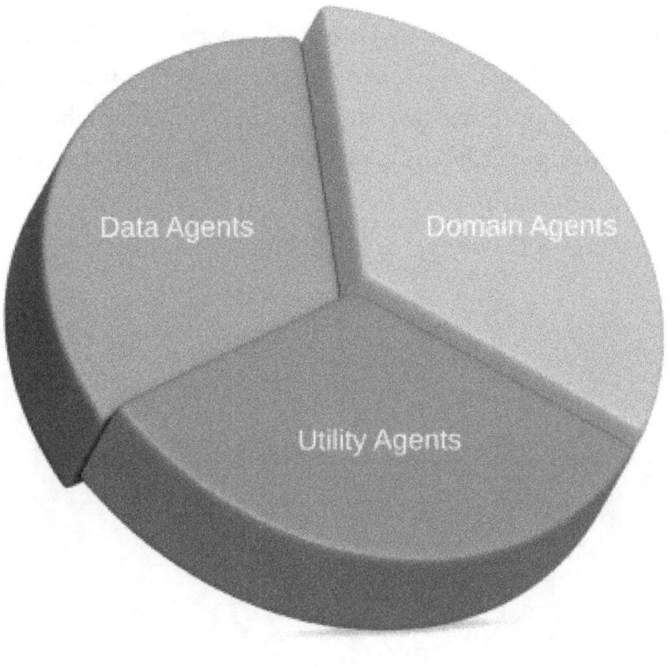

AI Agents

While AI Agents are conceptually categorized into Data Agents, Domain Agents, and Utility Agents, none of these agents individually holds the capability to address the complexity inherent in sophisticated business scenarios. Each type of agent fulfills a clearly defined role: Data Agents manage retrieval and structuring of vast repositories of information; Domain Agents interpret and apply specialized knowledge relevant to particular industries or functional areas; Utility Agents execute routine operational procedures, maintain consistent processes, and manage interactions among agents. However, isolating any one type of agent would significantly reduce effectiveness, as complex scenarios like those encountered in Events 1 through 4 inherently require the coordinated participation of all three agent categories.

For instance, consider the detailed regulatory scenario of Event 1 involving Fast Legs Corporation and RWJ Healthcare. A Data Agent alone, while capable of rapidly gathering and validating shipment records and financial transactions, lacks the specialized domain understanding necessary to interpret contractual complexities or regulatory stipulations such as the validation of 340B compliance via HRSA. Similarly, a Domain Agent specializing in healthcare regulation, although well-versed in applicable laws, would still require Data Agents to systematically and precisely retrieve accurate transaction-level details before domain expertise could meaningfully be applied.

Utility Agents fulfill an equally critical coordinating function, maintaining logical connections and clear communication between Data and Domain Agents. Without Utility Agents, the interaction between Data and Domain Agents would be disjointed, inefficient, or prone to errors. Utility Agents precisely orchestrate the flow of tasks, ensuring that data collected by Data Agents is timely and reliably delivered to Domain Agents for expert interpretation, then relayed accurately back into structured reporting formats.

When United Bank faced the fraud scenario in Event 4, the coordinated efforts of all three agent types were crucial. Data Agents extracted and systematically structured loan application information and agent associations. Domain Agents, familiar with financial fraud detection protocols and compliance standards, rapidly assessed fraudulent activities within their regulatory and operational contexts. Meanwhile, Utility Agents facilitated smooth exchanges between the other two agent types, allowing efficient handoffs of verified information and ensuring the clarity and consistency of final reporting.

Thus, the philosophy underlying effective AI Agent deployment acknowledges that complex operational challenges cannot be adequately addressed by any isolated agent category. Rather, success depends on the deliberate integration and coherent orchestration of Data, Domain, and Utility Agents. This purposeful synergy provides the comprehensive capability necessary for addressing real-world complexity effectively, confidently meeting the rigorous standards required in sophisticated business and regulatory environments.

Data Agents

Data Agents are specialized software components meticulously designed to manage precise data-related tasks, particularly involving retrieving, cleaning, validating, and preparing information from structured data sources. The role of a Data Agent is fundamentally practical: it gathers accurate and reliable information from databases, data warehouses, data lakes, and structured file repositories. These agents are carefully programmed to perform these data-centric operations with consistency, speed, and clarity, becoming a critical resource for efficiently managing complex data extraction and preparation tasks.

One defining capability of Data Agents is their ability to execute sophisticated data queries. These agents can proficiently utilize multiple querying languages and frameworks, including SQL for relational databases, PySpark for processing large-scale data sets in distributed computing environments, and even NoSQL querying languages for unstructured or semi-structured databases. For instance, a Data Agent may be assigned to query financial transactions from SAP using SQL, pulling specific details related to sales, discounts, or rebates for Event 1 involving Fast Legs Corporation and RWJ Healthcare. Alternatively, the same agent might leverage PySpark to quickly aggregate millions of records in a data lake, efficiently summarizing extensive transaction details.

Data Agents are also responsible for data cleaning an essential step that ensures the reliability of analytical outputs. Cleaning includes identifying incomplete records, removing or correcting inconsistent data entries, and validating data integrity based on clearly defined rules. A Data Agent might automatically detect and flag duplicate loan applications in the fraud investigation scenario for United Bank India (Event 4), ensuring accurate identification of fraudulent activities. Furthermore, these agents regularly monitor data quality, applying systematic checks for completeness, accuracy, timeliness, and consistency of data. Data quality evaluation might include identifying transactions with missing critical fields, detecting unusually high or low numeric values indicating potential data errors, or recognizing invalid date entries. Upon detection, Data Agents either correct the discrepancies automatically or clearly mark them for manual review, significantly enhancing data reliability.

Creating an effective Data Agent demands meticulous planning. Essential information must be explicitly programmed into the agent, including detailed database credentials such as usernames, secure passwords, IP addresses, database names, and port numbers to ensure seamless database connectivity. Additionally, the agent must be explicitly aware of the SQL dialect or "flavor" of databases it interacts with (such as MySQL, PostgreSQL, Oracle, SAP HANA, or SQL Server), as syntax differences may exist. The same detailed specification applies to PySpark setups, including clear instructions about clusters, memory settings, and file formats, ensuring optimal performance. Without precise setup information, Data Agents could face connectivity issues or unexpected errors, potentially leading to data retrieval failures or inaccuracies.

Several criteria determine a Data Agent's successful deployment and operation. Foremost among these criteria is accuracy the agent must consistently deliver reliable, correct data matching the original sources without distortion or loss of meaning. Performance speed is equally critical, as timely data retrieval enables swift analysis and decision-making. Additionally, flexibility and adaptability to manage diverse data queries and changing conditions such as fluctuating data volumes or rapidly evolving database schemas are important measures of effectiveness. Robust error managing and reporting capabilities, ensuring that users can rapidly diagnose and correct any issues, further enhance a Data Agent's operational success.

Data Agents rely heavily on meticulously defined metadata, developed during the data engineering phase, to identify precisely what data must be retrieved, how it should be structured, and what conditions apply. Metadata acts like a detailed roadmap, explicitly describing each data element's location, type, significance, and relationships with other elements. For example, structured metadata enables the agent to recognize "Net Sales" explicitly from transaction records or to clearly distinguish between 340B and non-340B transactions, as defined in Event 1. Filtering conditions embedded in metadata guide agents clearly: for instance, instructions such as "include only transactions within HRSA compliance dates" or "exclude loan records flagged as invalid" are readily available, enabling rapid, error-free querying. Without robust metadata, Data Agents would struggle to navigate complex data environments accurately or efficiently, potentially retrieving irrelevant or incorrect information.

In complex scenarios, Data Agents must seamlessly interpret and leverage the metadata provided by data engineering efforts. They carefully utilize this metadata to systematically apply filtering criteria, join conditions across multiple tables or sources, and specify precise data fields to extract. For instance, in the financial fraud scenario at United Bank India, metadata clearly describes attributes such as "Loan Application ID," "Customer ID," "Agent ID," "Loan Origination Date," and "Loan Amount," guiding the Data Agent to swiftly identify fraudulent loan patterns. Metadata also provides critical context for data elements such as transaction types, geographic locations, regulatory compliance markers enabling Data Agents to produce structured outputs ready for further domain-specific analysis.

In essence, Data Agents function effectively by meticulously following predefined, detailed instructions embedded in both their operational logic and comprehensive metadata descriptions. By executing complex data queries, systematically cleaning and validating data, and consistently maintaining high data quality, Data Agents form the indispensable core of data-centric activities. Their precise execution, governed by explicit metadata and clearly defined operational rules, provides organizations with the foundation necessary to reliably and confidently manage complex, data-intensive operations, setting the stage for successful, actionable results in all sophisticated analytical contexts.

Domain Agents

Domain Agents are highly specialized software components explicitly designed to address and manage detailed knowledge specific to particular industries, professional functions, or subject areas. Unlike Data Agents, whose primary responsibility revolves around the systematic retrieval and preparation of data, Domain Agents are created specifically to manage more sophisticated, context-sensitive tasks that require deep expertise in a certain field or domain. For example, in Event 2 (Bioncology Clinical Trial Fraud Investigation), Domain Agents would be equipped with extensive expertise in regulatory frameworks, clinical trial guidelines, and pharmaceutical compliance, enabling them to quickly identify mandatory regulatory steps and appropriate remedial measures following clinical trial data falsification.

To fulfill their role effectively, Domain Agents must incorporate detailed knowledge of specific regulatory guidelines, business rules, legal frameworks, or scientific standards directly relevant to their assigned tasks. A Domain Agent assigned to banking, such as in Event 3 (United Bank Interest Rate Adjustment Analysis), would have comprehensive familiarity with central bank monetary policy processes, including historical responses to economic events and current market standards for interpreting interest rate announcements. Similarly, a Domain Agent managing healthcare scenarios would possess expert-level understanding of regulatory agencies (such as FDA, EMA, HRSA), compliance mandates, clinical trial management practices, and healthcare-specific operational norms.

Domain Agents differ fundamentally from Human Digital Twins in that they are not attempting to mimic the nuanced cognitive reasoning or subjective understanding characteristic of human professionals. Instead, Domain Agents strictly apply predefined professional knowledge and operational guidelines consistently. While Human Digital Twins incorporate more subjective, situationally nuanced thinking, Domain Agents follow precise rules-based logic, ensuring accurate and consistent interpretation of domain-specific scenarios without subjective bias or emotional context. This clear boundary between nuanced cognitive interpretation and precise domain-specific logic ensures Domain Agents provide objective, dependable results aligned strictly with professional standards and compliance requirements.

Creating an effective Domain Agent involves embedding extensive domain knowledge explicitly into its operational logic. Such knowledge typically includes clearly defined domain-specific guidelines, regulatory compliance requirements, industry standards, and detailed scenario-managing procedures. For instance, in the financial fraud scenario of Event 4 (United Bank India), Domain Agents must have detailed instructions outlining regulatory mandates from India's RBI and Government of India, including precise fraud-management actions, mandated timelines for reporting, and specific legal procedures required to resolve detected incidents. This explicit embedding of domain-specific expertise ensures the Domain Agent consistently applies correct guidelines, minimizes risk of oversight, and provides accurate, comprehensive outputs suitable for regulatory submission and compliance audits.

Several critical criteria govern the successful implementation and deployment of Domain Agents. Foremost is domain accuracy the agent's capability to consistently and correctly interpret and apply detailed professional or regulatory guidelines. Reliability in producing outputs consistent with professional standards and regulatory compliance requirements is equally crucial. Moreover, Domain Agents must possess sufficient flexibility to accommodate evolving industry practices, regulatory updates, or changing business conditions without substantial reprogramming efforts. Robust and transparent error managing and reporting capabilities are essential, ensuring users can easily verify agent outputs, identify any discrepancies or omissions, and promptly correct potential inaccuracies.

Domain Agents heavily rely on clearly structured metadata developed during Data Engineering efforts. Metadata provides critical guidance about relevant data fields, relationships between data elements, and domain-specific context, enabling Domain Agents to swiftly identify precisely which information is required, how it relates to regulatory or business standards, and under what specific conditions domain-specific rules apply. For instance, metadata can help a healthcare-focused Domain Agent rapidly recognize the significance of "transaction date" and "covered entity status" when validating 340B compliance in Event 1 or guide a banking Domain Agent to accurately correlate "interest rate announcements" and "basis point adjustments" to monetary policy changes in Event 3.

Domain Agents apply metadata explicitly to perform precise filtering and interpretation of structured information. Clearly defined metadata allows these agents to rapidly verify whether specific regulatory conditions are met such as checking if clinical trial results align with FDA guidelines or ensuring financial loan practices strictly adhere to RBI-mandated compliance procedures. The metadata explicitly specifies detailed domain rules, operational criteria, regulatory standards, and business logic required for correct domain interpretation. Without robust metadata, Domain Agents could become inefficient, misapply guidelines, or produce inaccurate outputs, significantly diminishing their operational effectiveness.

Ultimately, Domain Agents represent a crucial component within the overall AI framework by providing precise, dependable application of domain-specific guidelines, rules, and standards. Their explicit, detailed programming allows organizations to consistently and accurately manage complex scenarios across healthcare, pharmaceuticals, finance, banking, and regulatory compliance. By leveraging carefully structured metadata from Data Engineering, Domain Agents execute clearly defined domain logic, ensuring accuracy, reliability, and operational effectiveness across even the most demanding real-world situations.

Utility Agents

Utility Agents are specialized software components explicitly created to manage operational tasks involving coordination, workflow management, and communication among various other agents, systems, and processes. Unlike Data Agents, which retrieve and process specific information, or Domain Agents, which apply specialized business or regulatory expertise, Utility Agents exclusively facilitate interactions, control sequences, monitor task completions, and report statuses. Their primary function is to systematically oversee the progression of activities and ensure that operational steps are executed according to explicitly defined workflows. They never perform analytical tasks such as data querying or regulatory interpretations themselves; instead, their responsibility revolves entirely around operational clarity, precise coordination, and efficient execution of processes.

The operational scope of Utility Agents is distinctively clear. They meticulously direct and monitor workflows, ensuring tasks initiated by Data or Domain Agents and external systems are executed properly, promptly, and in the correct sequence. For example, in Event 1 involving Fast Legs Corporation and RWJ Healthcare, once Data Agents have extracted relevant shipment data and confirmed transaction validity, Utility Agents ensure this output is promptly transferred to Domain Agents for regulatory interpretation and compliance verification. Similarly, Utility Agents systematically track notifications from external systems, like HRSA databases or central banking policy portals, and trigger appropriate downstream tasks as defined by operational procedures.

Creating effective Utility Agents demands detailed programming of workflow logic, clearly specifying task sequences, agent interactions, systems dependencies, and procedural rules. Operational logic explicitly describes which agent or system task must precede or follow another, including conditional triggers such as requiring completion of data validation before compliance analysis. For instance, during Event 4 (United Bank India Auto Loan Fraud Investigation), a Utility Agent explicitly confirms that Data Agents have fully completed the extraction of loan records and fraudulent patterns before allowing Domain Agents to initiate compliance assessments. Clear rules and explicit task definitions ensure Utility Agents maintain strict control over operational workflows without directly performing analytical functions themselves.

Success criteria for Utility Agents emphasize operational precision, clarity, and reliability. A successful Utility Agent consistently ensures tasks are initiated, monitored, and concluded in precisely defined sequences. Accuracy in task scheduling, clear monitoring of progress, timely completion, and prompt error identification or escalation are essential attributes. Robust reporting capabilities are similarly crucial, enabling human supervisors to quickly verify the status of ongoing processes and intervene when necessary. Additionally, flexibility to adjust operational sequences dynamically such as managing unexpected delays or rapid regulatory deadline shifts strengthens Utility Agents' effectiveness.

Utility Agents rely extensively on operational metadata generated during AI Orchestration, explicitly detailing how tasks should proceed, which agents or systems must interact, and under what conditions tasks are triggered. Operational metadata explicitly informs Utility Agents about sequences of agent and system tasks, clearly identifies dependencies between these tasks, and specifies exact triggers or conditions required for each operational step. For instance, in Event 3 (United Bank Interest Rate Analysis), operational metadata instructs Utility Agents explicitly when Data Agents complete news-feed monitoring, thereby clearly signaling Domain Agents to initiate interpretation of interest rate scenarios. Without precise operational metadata, Utility Agents would face considerable challenges maintaining clear, organized, and accurate workflow management.

Utility Agents leverage this clearly structured operational metadata to precisely manage and initiate workflows, ensuring correct sequencing, timing, and interactions between Data Agents, Domain Agents, and external systems. Explicit operational metadata allows Utility Agents to quickly identify dependencies such as confirming data extraction completion before compliance checks and to verify whether conditions required for subsequent task activation are met. Without explicitly defined operational metadata, Utility Agents would struggle significantly to orchestrate complex workflows accurately, increasing the risk of errors, delays, and operational confusion.

Ultimately, Utility Agents serve as critical operational managers within sophisticated agent-driven environments, maintaining meticulous oversight and coordination among various agents, systems, and business processes. Their explicit focus on clearly defined operational logic ensures reliable, precise, and organized execution of workflows, maintaining consistency and operational integrity across complex business scenarios. By strictly adhering to detailed operational metadata instructions from AI Orchestration, Utility Agents consistently deliver structured, dependable coordination and management of complex business processes essential for successful real-world AI implementations.

AI Agent Structure

The structure of an AI Agent must be meticulously defined and explicitly articulated to ensure clarity, accuracy, and operational consistency across complex environments. Just as metadata requires clearly structured, AI-readable descriptions, the AI Agent itself requires an equally clear and detailed definition of its capabilities, boundaries, operational responsibilities, and interactions. Precise definition removes ambiguity, clearly states what the Agent can and cannot do, ensures agents interact properly, and provides transparency for validation and verification processes.

First and foremost, clearly defining the scope of the AI Agent is critical. The agent's scope should explicitly articulate the tasks, queries, or calculations it is authorized and expected to perform, such as financial transaction validation, compliance checks, or market trend analysis. Equally important is explicitly stating what lies outside its operational boundaries for instance, specifying that an SQL Data Agent may only query structured financial data and explicitly stating it cannot directly interpret regulatory guidelines, which is strictly a Domain Agent responsibility. Defining this explicit boundary prevents overlap and confusion between different agent types.

The AI Agent's structure must also explicitly outline access control and system permissions. Clearly defined access details must include exact identification of systems and databases the agent is authorized to interact with, such as SAP for financial transactions or MDM for master data. Equally vital is explicitly declaring systems or databases the agent is strictly prohibited from accessing, providing a clear boundary of agent operations. Robust credential management strategies must be clearly incorporated this includes mechanisms such as secure key vault integration, secure token-based authentication, explicit managing of API keys, and credential rotation procedures. Clearly structured credential management instructions help maintain data security and ensure regulatory compliance.

To enhance transparency and ensure accountability, an effective AI Agent structure explicitly mandates comprehensive reasoning or logging behind each action it executes. For instance, when an SQL Query Agent generates queries, the agent should explicitly log or output clear, detailed reasoning about the generated query, including the exact tables selected, filter conditions applied, joins executed, and the rationale behind these choices. Similarly, if a Metrics Agent calculates business metrics, it should clearly document how each calculation was derived, including explicit definitions, formulas applied, and assumptions made. This detailed reasoning enables human operators to easily validate outputs, ensuring accuracy and accountability.

Explicit definitions around agent interactions and task orchestration must also be clearly incorporated. Each AI Agent must specify exactly how it will interact with other agents, clearly defining inputs, outputs, handoff conditions, and sequence management. For example, a Metrics Agent must explicitly state that it generates clearly defined calculation instructions, then precisely outlines how these instructions are transferred to an SQL Agent responsible for applying specific filters, groupings, and executing the calculation. Clearly defined and structured interaction logic ensures efficient and accurate cooperation between agents, reducing risk of operational gaps or miscommunication.

The optimal structural format for defining an AI Agent is typically YAML, as it provides clear, human-readable, structured documentation easily parsed by both humans and AI-driven systems. YAML enables explicit definition of agent capabilities, boundaries, credential management, action logging, agent interactions, and orchestration sequences. Structured clearly into sections such as "Agent Scope," "System Access and Credentials," "Task Definitions," "Interaction

Logic," and "Action Logging and Reasoning," YAML files provide clear, explicit definitions of an agent's entire operational framework in a format easily maintainable and transparent.

Additionally, an effective AI Agent structure should explicitly specify robust error-managing and escalation procedures. Clearly defined error conditions, troubleshooting guidelines, and escalation mechanisms must be outlined, detailing exactly how errors are identified, logged, communicated, and resolved. This explicit definition ensures rapid identification and mitigation of issues, maintaining operational reliability and consistency.

The structure should also incorporate explicit definitions of operational performance metrics, clearly outlining how success is measured such as accuracy rates, response times, and process completion rates. This provides clear visibility into agent effectiveness and supports continuous improvement. Further, explicit details about auditing and monitoring mechanisms should be included, clearly specifying how agents are regularly assessed, how performance logs are captured, and how compliance audits are managed.

In summary, clearly structured AI Agent definitions must comprehensively articulate agent scope, operational boundaries, credential management, action reasoning, interaction logic, error-managing procedures, performance metrics, and monitoring mechanisms. YAML provides an ideal format, offering explicit clarity and structured readability, supporting operational transparency and rigorous validation. By clearly defining each element of the agent's operational landscape, organizations ensure that AI Agents reliably execute their responsibilities with clarity, consistency, transparency, and robust accountability.

Structure Example - YAML

Agent:

name: "<Agent Name>" # (AI-readable)

type: "<Data | Domain | Utility>" # (AI-readable)

description: "<Concise, AI-readable explanation of agent purpose>" # (AI-readable)

Scope:

in scope: # (AI-readable)

- "<Explicit tasks agent is authorized to perform>" # (AI-readable)

out_of_scope: # (AI-readable)

- "<Explicit tasks agent is prohibited from performing>" # (AI-readable)

SystemAccess:

allowed_systems: # (AI-readable)

- system_name: "<System Name>" # (AI-readable)

system_type: "<Database | API | DocumentRepository | NewsFeed>" # (AI-readable)

credentials_reference: "<Secure vault or key management reference>" # (AI-readable)

access_level: "<ReadOnly | ReadWrite | ExecuteOnly>" # (AI-readable)

additional_details: "<Further AI-readable access specifications>" # (AI-readable)

restricted_systems: # (AI-readable)

- "<Systems explicitly disallowed for agent access>" # (AI-readable)

Tasks:

- task_id: "<Unique Task Identifier>" # (AI-readable)

description: "<Clear, AI-readable description of the task>" # (AI-readable)

task_type: "<DataRetrieval | DataValidation | DomainInterpretation | Coordination>" # (AI-readable)

inputs: # (AI-readable)

- "<Precisely defined inputs, format, and structure>" # (AI-readable)

outputs: # (AI-readable)

```
- "<Clearly defined expected outputs and formats>" # (AI-readable)
execution_conditions: # (AI-readable)
- "<Explicitly defined conditions to trigger task execution>" # (AI-readable)
Interactions:
upstream_agents: # (AI-readable)
- agent_name: "<Upstream agent name>" # (AI-readable)
interaction_details: "<AI-readable description of inputs received>" # (AI-readable)
downstream_agents: # (AI-readable)
- agent_name: "<Downstream agent name>" # (AI-readable)
interaction_details: "<AI-readable description of outputs provided>" # (AI-readable)
ActionReasoning:
logging_required: true # (AI-readable)
log_detail_level: "<Brief | Detailed | Verbose>" # (AI-readable)
logs_storage: "<Secure log storage location>" # (AI-readable)
reasoning_format: "<PlainText | JSON | XML>" # (AI-readable)
MetadataUsage:
metadata_sources: # (AI-readable)
- "<Clearly defined sources of metadata (operational, structural)>" # (AI-readable)
metadata_application: # (AI-readable)
- "<Clearly stated use of metadata for queries, filtering, and orchestration>" # (AI-readable)
ErrorHandling:
error_detection_methods: # (AI-readable)
- "<Explicitly defined methods to detect errors>" # (AI-readable)
escalation_procedures: # (AI-readable)
- "<Defined process for escalation when errors occur>" # (AI-readable)
notification_channels: # (AI-readable)
- "<Channels or methods to report errors (email, API notifications)>" # (AI-readable)
```

PerformanceMetrics:

success_criteria: # (AI-readable)

- "<Metrics defining agent's performance success>" # (AI-readable)

monitoring_mechanism: "<Clearly defined mechanism for monitoring agent performance>" # (AI-readable)

audit_logs: "<Location for secure storage of performance and audit logs>" # (AI-readable)

VersionControl:

agent_version: "<Explicit version identifier>" # (AI-readable)

version_update_date: "<Date of last update>" # (AI-readable)

change_description: "<AI-readable summary of changes made>" # (AI-readable)

Data Agent Example – SQL Agent

Agent:

name: "Universal_SQL_Query_Agent" # (AI-readable) Clearly identifies the agent uniquely to the AI model.

type: "Data" # (AI-readable) Defines the agent category explicitly for task-specific logic.

description: "Generates accurate and optimized SQL queries dynamically across multiple databases including Redshift, SAP HANA, SQL Server, and Trino. It explicitly interprets AI-readable metadata, translating detailed instructions into precise, executable database-specific queries. Queries follow metadata instructions for exact table selections, column identifications, filter criteria, joins, groupings, and aggregations, ensuring data accuracy, consistency, and alignment with analytical requirements." # (AI-readable) Provides detailed agent scope for precise LLM understanding.

Scope:

in_scope: # (AI-readable) Explicitly instructs the AI model on allowed tasks.

- "Generate SQL queries dynamically tailored to Redshift, SAP HANA, SQL Server, and Trino."

- "Interpret AI-readable metadata to precisely identify columns, joins, and filters."

- "Create SQL aggregations, groupings, and sorting strictly per metadata instructions."

out_of_scope: # (AI-readable) Explicitly instructs the AI model on prohibited tasks.

- "Interpret regulatory rules or perform domain-specific analytical calculations."

- "Execute or commit changes directly to databases."

SystemAccess:

allowed_systems: # (AI-readable) Clearly lists databases this agent can access for LLM reference.

- system_name: "AWS_Redshift_Production" # (AI-readable) Clearly identifies the database system for the LLM.

system_type: "Database" # (AI-readable) Explicit system category for LLM interpretation.

credentials_reference: "AWS IAM roles using temporary security credentials with rotating tokens via AWS Secrets Manager" # (AI-readable) Clearly informs LLM that credential management is managed externally and securely.

access_level: "ReadOnly" # (AI-readable) Specifies explicitly the limitations for the agent to maintain security.

additional_details: "Query must strictly adhere to Redshift SQL syntax, including correct managing of distribution keys and optimized joins." # (AI-readable) LLM explicitly instructed to use only Redshift SQL syntax when generating queries for this database.

- system_name: "SAP_HANA_ERP_DB" # (AI-readable) Explicit database name for LLM.

system_type: "Database" # (AI-readable) Explicit database type definition.

credentials_reference: "SAP Single Sign-On (SSO) tokens provided through secure SAML authentication process" # (AI-readable) Credential management explanation.

access_level: "ReadOnly" # (AI-readable) Defines explicit permission boundary.

additional_details: "Use SAP HANA-specific SQL syntax and functions; manage schemas and namespaces explicitly per metadata instructions." # (AI-readable) LLM explicitly instructed to apply SAP HANA SQL syntax only.

- system_name: "SQL_Server_Finance_DB" # (AI-readable) Explicit naming helps the LLM clearly target the correct database.

system_type: "Database" # (AI-readable) Explicit type identification.

credentials_reference: "Azure Active Directory managed identities integrated via Azure Key Vault" # (AI-readable) Credential security clearly defined for LLM awareness.

access_level: "ReadOnly" # (AI-readable) Permission limitations explicitly stated.

additional_details: "Queries must conform to T-SQL dialect; ensure proper schema and database references based on metadata." # (AI-readable) LLM explicitly informed to write T-SQL syntax queries only.

- system_name: "Trino_Query_Engine" # (AI-readable) Provides exact system identification.

system_type: "Database" # (AI-readable) Explicit categorization for clarity.

credentials_reference: "OAuth tokens generated and managed through secure API authentication" # (AI-readable) Clear credential management instructions for LLM context.

access_level: "ReadOnly" # (AI-readable) Defines explicit limitations for system interactions.

additional_details: "Use ANSI-standard SQL dialect compatible with Trino, clearly defined schema and catalog instructions per metadata." # (AI-readable) Explicit instruction that the LLM generates only ANSI-standard SQL syntax compatible with Trino.

Tasks:

- task_id: "Generate_SQL_Query" # (AI-readable) Clearly identifies the task for agent execution.

description: "Use explicit AI-readable metadata instructions to dynamically build accurate, optimized SQL queries, tailored for specified databases, clearly identifying correct columns, tables, joins, groupings, aggregations, sorting and filtering criteria." # (AI-readable) Provides detailed task description explicitly guiding LLM logic.

task_type: "DataRetrieval" # (AI-readable) Defines the task category explicitly.

inputs: # (AI-readable, Metadata usage) Clearly instructs LLM to strictly follow metadata inputs.

- "AI-readable metadata containing explicit definitions of databases, schemas, tables, column names, joins, precise filter conditions, and aggregation instructions." # (AI-readable, Metadata usage) Clearly instructs LLM how metadata should drive query structure and conditions.

outputs: # (AI-readable) Clearly instructs LLM about expected deliverable format.

- "Validated and executable SQL query strings, precisely tailored to specified databases, strictly adhering to metadata instructions." # (AI-readable) Defines explicit output expectations for the LLM.

execution_conditions: # (AI-readable) Clearly instructs the LLM under which conditions to proceed with task execution.

- "Complete and validated metadata instructions available specifying target database, columns, filters, joins, grouping, and aggregation logic." # (AI-readable, Metadata usage) LLM explicitly required to verify metadata completeness before proceeding.

Interactions:

upstream_agents: # (AI-readable) Explicitly details dependencies for LLM clarity.

- agent_name: "Business_Metrics_Definition_Agent" # (AI-readable) Clearly defines upstream dependency explicitly for LLM.

interaction_details: "Receives clear, AI-readable instructions for column selection, metric calculations, filter logic, grouping, and sorting criteria." # (AI-readable) Explicitly describes the type of input the LLM receives from upstream agent.

downstream_agents: # (AI-readable) Explicitly details outputs to LLM-defined agents.

- agent_name: "SQL_Execution_and_Validation_Agent" # (AI-readable) Clearly defines downstream agent explicitly for LLM reference.

interaction_details: "Passes precisely formatted and validated database-specific SQL queries ready for secure execution." # (AI-readable) Explicitly defines how LLM-generated queries are handed off downstream.

ActionReasoning:

logging_required: true # (AI-readable) LLM explicitly informed that logging is mandatory for transparency and auditability.

log_detail_level: "Detailed" # (AI-readable) Defines log detail explicitly for LLM reference.

logs_storage: "SecureLogs/UniversalSQLAgentLogs" # (AI-readable) Explicit location provided for LLM log outputs.

reasoning_format: "PlainText" # (AI-readable) Explicit formatting guidance for LLM-generated explanations.

MetadataUsage:

metadata_sources: # (AI-readable, Metadata usage) LLM explicitly informed of metadata sources.

- "AI_Readable_Metadata/DataQueriesDefinitions" # (AI-readable, Metadata usage) Provides explicit reference for the LLM to interpret and use.

metadata_application: # (AI-readable, Metadata usage) Explicitly instructs LLM how to use provided metadata.

- "Explicitly uses metadata to clearly identify database types, tables, schemas, columns, join logic, grouping, sorting, precise aggregation methods, and filtering conditions for accurate SQL query generation." # (AI-readable, Metadata usage) Defines metadata role explicitly in LLM-generated queries.

- "Strictly interprets metadata-defined logical conditions to accurately apply database-specific syntax for WHERE clauses, JOINs, GROUP BY statements, and ORDER BY clauses." # (AI-readable, Metadata usage) Provides explicit metadata application guidance to the LLM for accurate SQL generation.

ErrorHandling:

error_detection_methods: # (AI-readable) Defines explicit error detection guidelines for the LLM.

- "Automated syntax validation checks for SQL dialect compliance prior to query finalization." # (AI-readable) Clearly instructs LLM to include syntax validation.

- "Pre-execution metadata-based checks confirming that columns and tables referenced in the query are valid and consistent with schema." # (AI-readable, Metadata usage) LLM explicitly instructed to validate queries against metadata before finalizing.

escalation_procedures: # (AI-readable) Explicitly informs LLM of procedures in case of errors.

- "Immediate escalation via automated alerts to Database Administrators and Data Architects upon detecting invalid references or syntax errors." # (AI-readable) Defines explicit escalation clearly for the LLM.

notification_channels: # (AI-readable) Explicitly defines communication channels for error notifications.

- "Real-time system alerts, Slack channel notifications, and immediate email notifications to responsible Database and Data Management teams." # (AI-readable) Defines clear notification protocols explicitly for LLM error managing.

Domain Agent - Metrics Definition

Agent:

name: "Business_Metrics_Definition_Agent" # (AI-readable) Explicit unique identifier enabling clear LLM recognition.

type: "Domain" # (AI-readable) Clearly defines agent as Domain-specific for LLM understanding.

description: "Defines explicit standalone calculation logic for key business metrics: Sum, Average (Avg), Market Share, Year-over-Year (YoY) growth, and Quarter-over-Quarter (QoQ) growth. Metrics explicitly defined in reference to current system date, clearly articulating specific columns, conditions, and Total Market definitions. Provides precise logic to guide downstream SQL agents accurately, explicitly preventing ambiguity or hallucinations." # (AI-readable) Clearly informs LLM of explicit agent responsibilities.

Scope:

in_scope: # (AI-readable) Explicitly instructs LLM about permitted activities.

- "Clearly define explicit calculation logic for Sum, Avg, Market Share, YoY growth, QoQ growth."

- "Explicitly define year and quarter references based strictly on the current system date (e.g., Y0=current calendar year)."

- "Clearly articulate precise definitions and conditions for Total Market within each metric calculation."

out_of_scope: # (AI-readable) Explicitly defines tasks prohibited for LLM clarity.

- "Direct database queries or data extraction tasks."

- "Perform regulatory interpretations or operational management tasks."

SystemAccess:

allowed_systems: # (AI-readable) Clearly defines systems accessible to the agent.

- system_name: "Metrics_Definition_Documentation_Repository" # (AI-readable) Explicit reference for LLM identification.

system_type: "DocumentRepository" # (AI-readable) Clear categorization for LLM reference.

credentials_reference: "Secured via internal AD-based SSO credentials." # (AI-readable) Explicit credential management clearly indicated.

access_level: "ReadOnly" # (AI-readable) Explicit permission boundaries clearly defined.

additional_details: "Contains explicitly documented definitions of all business metric calculation logics and precise timeframe references." # (AI-readable) Explicitly informs LLM what type of documentation the agent can access.

Tasks:

- task_id: "Define_Metrics_Calculation_Logic" # (AI-readable) Explicitly identified task for LLM clarity.

description: "Clearly defines explicit standalone logic for Sum, Avg, Market Share, YoY, QoQ metrics with precise timeframe references based on current system date, explicit column specifications, and clear Total Market definitions for SQL query accuracy." # (AI-readable) Explicitly instructs LLM on task details.

task_type: "DomainInterpretation" # (AI-readable) Explicitly defines the nature of the task.

inputs: # (AI-readable) Clearly instructs LLM on explicit input type.

- "Explicit business definitions clearly specifying metric details, timeframe references, and business conditions provided by domain experts." # (AI-readable) Clear definition of inputs for LLM clarity.

outputs: # (AI-readable) Clearly instructs LLM about explicit output deliverables.

- "Explicitly defined calculation logic documentation for each metric, clearly understandable and executable by downstream SQL agents." # (AI-readable) Explicitly defines agent's expected outputs.

execution_conditions: # (AI-readable) Explicitly instructs LLM regarding task prerequisites.

- "Validated and explicitly provided business context, timeframe definitions, and metric-specific details." # (AI-readable) Clear conditions before task execution.

Explicit_Calculation_Logic: # (AI-readable) Explicit, standalone logic definitions guiding LLM to avoid hallucination:

Sum: "Explicitly calculate by adding numeric values within clearly defined columns, applying explicit filter conditions for a user-defined period. For example, SUM(Sales) WHERE Period = <User_Specified_Period>. # (AI-readable) The LLM explicitly understands that the specific period will be provided by the user in the prompt. If no period is provided, explicitly prompt the user to specify this before generating."

Average (Avg): "Explicitly calculate by dividing the sum of defined numeric values by the count of non-null records within a clearly specified period. For example, AVG(Sales) = SUM(Sales) / COUNT(Sales) WHERE Period = <User_Specified_Period>. # (AI-readable) The LLM explicitly recognizes the period as a required parameter from user prompts. If the user omits this, explicitly prompt the user to define the period before proceeding."

Market_Share: "Explicitly calculate as (Entity Sales for the specified period / Total Sales of defined industry, region, or market for the same period) * 100. For example, (Entity Sales WHERE Period = <User_Specified_Period>) / (Total Sales of <User_Specified_Industry_or_Region_or_Market> WHERE Period = <User_Specified_Period>) * 100. # (AI-readable) The LLM explicitly understands that period, industry, region, or market details must be provided by the user in the prompt. If any details are missing, explicitly prompt the user for this information before generating."

Year_over_Year_Growth (YoY): "Explicitly calculate as ((Sales_Y0 - Sales_Y-1) / Sales_Y-1) * 100. Clearly define Y0 as current calendar year (YEAR(TRANSACTION_DATE)), Y-1 as previous calendar year (YEAR(TRANSACTION_DATE)-1), explicitly instructing SQL agent on timeframe conditions." # (AI-readable) Explicitly provides timeframe logic preventing LLM hallucination.

Quarter_over_Quarter_Growth (QoQ): "Explicitly calculate as ((Sales for the current calendar quarter - Sales for the immediately preceding calendar quarter) / Sales for the immediately preceding calendar quarter) * 100. For example: ((SUM(Sales) WHERE Quarter = Quarter(TRANSACTION_DATE) AND Year =

Year(TRANSACTION_DATE)) - (SUM(Sales) WHERE Quarter = Quarter(TRANSACTION_DATE)-1, adjusting Year as necessary)) / (SUM(Sales) WHERE Quarter = Quarter(TRANSACTION_DATE)-1, adjusting Year as necessary) * 100. # (AI-readable) The LLM explicitly understands that quarter references strictly relate to the calendar quarter of the current system date, clearly adjusting the year when evaluating the previous quarter."

Interactions:

upstream_agents: # (AI-readable) Clearly defines explicit agent interactions for LLM.

- agent_name: "Business_Context_Input_Agent" # (AI-readable) Clearly identified agent providing initial metric context.

interaction_details: "Receives explicit definitions of business requirements, clearly specifying metric contexts, column usage, timeframe definitions (Y0, Y-1, Q0, Q-1)." # (AI-readable) Explicitly defines upstream input clearly for LLM understanding.

downstream_agents: # (AI-readable) Clearly defines explicit agent interactions downstream.

- agent_name: "Universal_SQL_Query_Agent" # (AI-readable) Clearly identified downstream SQL agent.

interaction_details: "Provides explicitly defined, standalone metric calculation logic, clearly specifying exact columns, timeframe references, and explicit conditions ensuring SQL accuracy." # (AI-readable) Explicitly instructs LLM on downstream usage of metric definitions.

ActionReasoning:

logging_required: true # (AI-readable) Explicitly mandates LLM logging for auditability.

log_detail_level: "Detailed" # (AI-readable) Explicitly defines level of detail for action logs.

logs_storage: "SecureLogs/MetricsDefinitionAgentLogs" # (AI-readable) Explicit location defined for action logging.

reasoning_format: "PlainText" # (AI-readable) Explicit format instruction for LLM-generated logs.

ErrorHandling:

error_detection_methods: # (AI-readable) Explicitly defines LLM error detection methods.

- "Explicit verification of calculation logic for mathematical correctness, column validity, and explicit timeframe accuracy prior to definition finalization." # (AI-readable) Explicitly instructs LLM to check logic accuracy.

escalation_procedures: # (AI-readable) Explicitly defines error escalation clearly for LLM.

- "Immediate escalation via system notifications to Domain Experts and Business Analysts upon logic inconsistency detection." # (AI-readable) Explicitly guides LLM escalation.

notification_channels: # (AI-readable) Explicit communication protocols defined clearly.

- "Automated system alerts, immediate email notifications, and real-time Slack messages to domain experts and data management teams." # (AI-readable) Clearly informs LLM how to communicate errors.

PerformanceMetrics:

success_criteria: # (AI-readable) Explicitly defines criteria for success for LLM validation.

- "100% accuracy in clearly defined metric logic validated by domain experts."

- "Clear, explicit metric definitions enabling flawless execution by downstream SQL agents."

monitoring_mechanism: "Routine expert reviews and automated mathematical logic consistency checks." # (AI-readable)

audit_logs: "SecureLogs/MetricAgentAuditLogs" # (AI-readable)

VersionControl:

agent_version: "v1.1.0" # (AI-readable)

version_update_date: "2025-04-18" # (AI-readable)

change_description: "Updated explicitly defined metric calculation logic for Sum, Avg, Market Share, YoY, QoQ, clearly referencing current system date for year and quarter, and precisely defining Total Market conditions explicitly." # (AI-readable)

Utility Agent – RBAC

Agent:

name: "RBAC_User_Access_Validation_Agent" # (AI-readable) Explicit agent identification for precise LLM recognition.

type: "Utility" # (AI-readable) Explicitly categorized as Utility agent for task-specific logic.

description: "Explicitly validates user access permissions for sensitive data, clearly identifying whether users have appropriate authorization to access requested resources. Manages multiple scenarios explicitly, including successful access, access denial, additional information required, managerial approvals, and temporary restricted access, ensuring users receive explicit guidance or notifications to resolve access-related queries." # (AI-readable) Clearly defines the agent's explicit scope and functionality.

Scope:

in_scope: # (AI-readable) Clearly instructs the LLM on authorized agent tasks.

- "Explicit validation of user access to sensitive or restricted data."

- "Clearly defined scenarios: access granted, access denied, additional information required, approval required."

- "Provide explicit user notifications for access validation outcomes."

out_of_scope: # (AI-readable) Clearly instructs the LLM on tasks explicitly outside agent boundaries.

- "Performing data queries, direct SQL, or metric calculations."

- "Directly modifying or assigning permissions."

SystemAccess:

allowed_systems: # (AI-readable) Explicitly defines systems accessible for user-role validation.

- system_name: "Enterprise_User_Permissions_DB" # (AI-readable) Explicit reference for permissions system.

system_type: "RoleManagementSystem" # (AI-readable) Clearly categorizes system for access validation tasks.

credentials_reference: "Secured via internal AD-based authentication with MFA enabled." # (AI-readable) Credential management explicitly defined.

access_level: "ReadOnly" # (AI-readable) Explicitly limits agent access permissions.

additional_details: "System explicitly contains roles, permissions, managerial hierarchies, and user access logs." # (AI-readable) Explicit LLM instructions regarding system contents.

Tasks:

- task_id: "Validate_User_Access_Request" # (AI-readable) Explicit unique identifier for clear LLM task recognition.

description: "Explicitly validates user access requests against clearly defined roles and permissions. Provides explicit outcomes based on RBAC validation: success, denial, more information required, or managerial approval." # (AI-readable) Clearly instructs the LLM on validation task details.

task_type: "AccessValidation" # (AI-readable) Explicitly categorizes the task clearly.

inputs: # (AI-readable)

- "Explicit user ID, requested data resource, and specific action the user wishes to perform." # (AI-readable) Clearly instructs the LLM on required input specifics.

outputs: # (AI-readable)

- "Explicit notification of access result: access granted, access denied, additional information requested, managerial approval required, temporary restriction notice." # (AI-readable) Clearly instructs LLM regarding explicit output formats.

execution_conditions: # (AI-readable)

- "User explicitly submits access request with clearly defined resource details and desired action." # (AI-readable) Explicit conditions required for task initiation.

Explicit_Scenarios: # (AI-readable) Clearly defined scenarios to avoid ambiguity for the LLM:

- scenario: "Access Granted"

condition: "User has explicitly defined permissions matching the requested resource and action."

action: "Explicitly inform user: 'Access granted. You have the required permissions for the requested data and action.'"

- scenario: "Access Denied"

condition: "User explicitly lacks necessary permissions for requested resource or action."

action: "Explicitly inform user: 'Access denied. You do not have permissions to access this resource or perform this action. Please contact your system administrator.'"

- scenario: "Additional Information Required"

condition: "User request lacks explicit clarity or sufficient detail on the requested resource or intended action."

action: "Explicitly inform user: 'More information required. Please explicitly clarify the resource name, purpose, and intended action for further validation.'"

- scenario: "Managerial Approval Required"

condition: "Requested resource or action explicitly requires managerial or supervisory approval as per RBAC policy."

action: "Explicitly inform user: 'Managerial approval required. Please obtain explicit approval from your direct manager or supervisor and submit documented approval for processing.'"

- scenario: "Temporary Restriction Notice"

condition: "Requested resource temporarily restricted due to explicit audit, compliance review, or operational policy."

action: "Explicitly inform user: 'Temporary restriction in place. The requested resource is temporarily restricted due to ongoing audits or compliance reviews. Please contact the compliance team for further assistance.'"

Interactions:

upstream_agents: # (AI-readable) Clearly instructs LLM on agent input interactions.

- agent_name: "User_Request_Intake_Agent" # (AI-readable) Clearly defined upstream agent.

interaction_details: "Receives explicit user access requests with clear user identification, resource names, and requested actions." # (AI-readable) Explicitly instructs LLM on upstream interaction details.

downstream_agents: # (AI-readable) Clearly instructs LLM on agent output interactions.

- agent_name: "User_Notification_Agent" # (AI-readable) Clearly defined downstream notification agent.

interaction_details: "Explicitly passes user access validation results to notify users regarding the outcome of their access requests." # (AI-readable) Explicitly instructs LLM on downstream interaction specifics.

ActionReasoning:

logging_required: true # (AI-readable) Explicitly instructs mandatory logging for LLM actions.

log_detail_level: "Detailed" # (AI-readable) Explicitly defines detailed logging.

logs_storage: "SecureLogs/RBACAgentActionLogs" # (AI-readable) Clearly defines secure log storage location.

reasoning_format: "PlainText" # (AI-readable) Explicit instruction for log formatting.

ErrorHandling:

error_detection_methods: # (AI-readable) Explicitly instructs LLM on methods to detect task errors.

- "Explicit validation of user identity, resource existence, and action clarity prior to access evaluation." # (AI-readable) Clearly instructs on validation methods.

escalation_procedures: # (AI-readable) Explicitly instructs LLM on escalation in error scenarios.

- "Explicit immediate escalation via automated notifications to RBAC System Administrators upon detection of inconsistencies or access violations." # (AI-readable)

notification_channels: # (AI-readable) Clearly instructs LLM on explicit communication channels.

- "Real-time alerts, automated email notifications, and Slack messages to RBAC administration teams." # (AI-readable)

PerformanceMetrics:

success_criteria: # (AI-readable) Explicit criteria clearly defined for performance evaluation.

- "100% accuracy in explicitly validating user access permissions per defined RBAC policies."

- "Immediate explicit notification provided for every access request outcome."

monitoring_mechanism: "Routine compliance audits and automated consistency checks." # (AI-readable)

audit_logs: "SecureLogs/RBACAgentAuditLogs" # (AI-readable)

VersionControl:

agent_version: "v1.0.0" # (AI-readable)

version_update_date: "2025-04-18" # (AI-readable)

change_description: "Initial explicit definition of RBAC agent covering all critical user access validation scenarios: access success, denial, additional information request, managerial approval required, and temporary restrictions explicitly detailed." # (AI-readable)

The agent structures provided above Universal SQL Query Agent, Business Metrics Definition Agent, and RBAC User Access Validation Agent are illustrative samples designed primarily to offer explicit guidelines for creating AI-readable instructions. In real-world, production-grade environments, designing effective AI Agents demands a meticulous architectural approach that goes significantly beyond these simplified representations. The deployment and operation of agents in complex enterprise ecosystems must reflect a deep understanding of the organization's specific business needs, technical capabilities, resource availability, and operational philosophies. Furthermore, robust AI Agent architecture encompasses several additional dimensions such as scalability requirements, error management strategies, compliance with internal governance frameworks, regulatory standards, data security mandates, and integration with existing enterprise applications and workflows.

An essential aspect of comprehensive AI Agent design involves clearly defining the organization's philosophy. This philosophy encompasses the guiding principles, values, and strategic objectives that shape how AI technologies should operate within organizational boundaries. For example, organizations prioritizing transparency and auditability might emphasize agents with highly detailed action logging and comprehensive reasoning documentation. Similarly, an organization focused on strict regulatory compliance will design agents explicitly with meticulous error-detection protocols, structured escalation procedures, and compliance-centric validation mechanisms. Moreover, the organization's overall data governance policies, ethical guidelines for AI use, principles of fairness, accountability, and the company's risk tolerance levels significantly influence how agents are architected, implemented, and operationally managed.

Additionally, effective AI Agent architecture demands a detailed understanding of the organization's technical landscape. This includes a thorough assessment of existing database infrastructures, data integration strategies, enterprise metadata management systems, and security protocols. Real-world agents must be designed not only to achieve immediate functional goals but also to seamlessly operate across diverse technical environments. Thus, real production-grade agents explicitly define credential management protocols, system access hierarchies, secure interaction patterns, and precise integration points with various internal and external systems, taking into consideration long-term maintainability, operational reliability, and future scalability.

It is critical to recognize that the specific agent interactions described in the earlier illustrative YAML structures are purely examples demonstrating potential communication and coordination patterns. In actual enterprise production systems, routing tasks between agents such as task sequencing, status checks, dependency validations, and communication is explicitly managed by an advanced and sophisticated management framework known as AI Agent Orchestration. AI Agent Orchestration refers to the systematic coordination, governance, and control of multiple interacting agents, clearly defining how each agent should interact, sequence tasks, exchange data, and maintain operational coherence. Unlike simple linear interactions, production-grade agent orchestrations involve complex workflows, conditional branching logic, error-managing mechanisms, performance tracking, resource balancing, and dynamic scaling.

AI Agent Orchestration explicitly defines and manages dependencies among multiple AI agents. It ensures that Data, Domain, and Utility agents collaborate effectively, enforcing strict adherence to business rules, access controls, and operational policies. Additionally, orchestration mechanisms provide sophisticated error detection, remediation strategies, detailed performance metrics, real-time status tracking, and automated notifications. The orchestration framework explicitly assigns responsibilities, sequences tasks logically, dynamically adapts to changing conditions, and ensures resilience and robustness in complex operational scenarios. Furthermore, it offers comprehensive auditing capabilities, tracking each agent's actions, decisions, and communication flows, thus providing clear visibility and transparency into the entire agent ecosystem.

The detailed architecture, implementation patterns, best practices, and operational methodologies associated with AI Agent Orchestration are extensive and complex. Therefore, the upcoming volume in this educational series will explicitly focus on AI Agent Orchestration. It will comprehensively detail how enterprise-grade agent orchestration is systematically designed, clearly structured, operationally managed, and governed. Readers will gain insights into practical methods, architectural considerations, orchestration tools, interaction frameworks, error management strategies, compliance mechanisms, and performance optimization techniques necessary to deploy sophisticated, enterprise-ready AI Agent systems effectively.

RAG and NLP to SQL

Retrieval-Augmented Generation (RAG) and NLP-to-SQL Agents represent two distinct yet interrelated types of Data Agents, each specifically designed to manage different forms of enterprise knowledge. Both play essential roles in modern data-driven environments, particularly within complex business scenarios that require comprehensive data integration from both structured and unstructured data sources.

RAG Agents specialize in managing and interacting with unstructured text-based information sources such as contracts, policies, regulatory documents, news articles, and research publications. These agents leverage sophisticated natural language processing (NLP) techniques, embedding methods, semantic search, and large language models (LLMs) to intelligently retrieve and synthesize relevant textual data. In a typical workflow, a RAG Agent takes a user's query, converts it into a semantic representation, and then retrieves the most contextually relevant document snippets or sections from large document repositories. This retrieved information provides essential contextual grounding, enabling the agent to produce precise and contextually appropriate responses. The retrieval and generation process within RAG is explicitly designed to address the common pitfalls of generative models, such as hallucinations and inaccuracies, by explicitly ensuring responses are anchored to verified source documents.

Conversely, NLP-to-SQL Agents address the structured data dimension, specifically interacting with databases, data warehouses, and data lakes containing clearly defined tables, columns, relationships, and schemas. These agents translate natural language questions or business instructions directly into accurate and executable SQL statements. To perform this task reliably, NLP-to-SQL Agents rely explicitly on detailed metadata that clearly describes the underlying database structures and defines explicit mappings between natural language terms and database columns. Advanced NLP techniques, combined with semantic parsing and metadata interpretation, enable these agents to generate precise, validated, and highly optimized SQL queries. This capability greatly accelerates data retrieval, significantly reduces manual query writing efforts, and ensures that business users without deep technical SQL expertise can reliably access critical data.

In sophisticated, real-world scenarios such as contract performance analyses exemplified by the scenario involving Fast Legs Corporation and RWJ Healthcare RAG and NLP-to-SQL Agents function collaboratively, leveraging their respective strengths. For instance, the RAG Agent explicitly retrieves and synthesizes key contractual terms, conditions, and compliance rules from PDF-based documents, clearly defining crucial elements such as pricing terms, discount conditions, or regulatory compliance requirements. Simultaneously, the NLP-to-SQL Agent explicitly uses this extracted context to dynamically construct and execute database queries against transactional databases, applying precise aggregation logic, filters, joins, and conditions defined by the RAG-retrieved contractual details. Together, these agents enable a highly integrated and accurate analytical process, seamlessly connecting unstructured contractual clauses with structured transactional data, yielding comprehensive insights into contract performance, compliance statuses, and financial impacts.

This integrated agent approach significantly enhances the speed, accuracy, and depth of analysis possible within modern enterprise environments. By explicitly combining RAG and NLP-to-SQL capabilities, businesses achieve streamlined access to holistic insights that were traditionally difficult, time-consuming, or error-prone to compile manually. For example, in scenarios involving regulatory compliance audits, pharmaceutical clinical trial evaluations, or financial investigations, this integrated approach clearly enables rapid identification of critical issues, accurate cross-validation of data points, and swift generation of compliant, detailed reports.

Given the inherent complexity, advanced capabilities, and strategic importance of these specialized Data Agents, the architectural design, deployment strategies, and operational methodologies required for effective implementation are highly nuanced. Consequently, the upcoming volume in this educational series will be exclusively dedicated to exploring RAG and NLP-to-SQL Agents in significant depth. This dedicated volume will explicitly detail advanced architectural frameworks, metadata design principles, NLP techniques, semantic embedding methods, SQL generation best practices, error managing mechanisms, compliance considerations, agent orchestration strategies, and practical, real-world demonstrations. Readers will gain explicit, actionable knowledge on systematically deploying, integrating, and managing these advanced Data Agents, enabling their organizations to realize the full strategic value of comprehensive, AI-driven data integration and analysis.

AI Agents by Events

Event 1 – Fast Legs & RWJ Contract Analysis

- **SQL Query Agent** – pulls six-quarter shipment, discount, and sales facts.
- **HRSA Validation API Agent** – verifies 340B locations against daily CE list.
- **Contract RAG Agent** – extracts pricing and rebate clauses from the PDF.
- **Metrics Definition Agent** – standardises Sum, Avg, QoQ calculations.
- **340B Pricing Compliance Agent** – checks discount ceilings and duplicate rules.
- **RBAC Agent** – guards SAP and contract content.

Event 2 – Bioncology Trial Fraud

- **Clinical-Document RAG Agent** – retrieves investigator contracts and protocol files.
- **Trial-Registry Data Agent** – gathers structured enrolment and endpoint records.
- **Clinical Regulatory Compliance Agent** – maps breaches to FDA / ICH timelines.
- **Risk Mitigation Strategy Agent** – proposes PI suspension and data-lock steps.
- **SQL Update Agent** – writes back to the trial-master database, adding audit comments, revoking the PI's KOL status, and flagging the investigator as black-listed for future studies.
- **RBAC Agent** – limits dossier access to authorized QA, legal, and PV staff.

Event 3 – United Bank Rate-Cut Rumors

- **Analyst-News RAG Agent** – mines Bloomberg and central-bank commentary.
- **Exposure-SQL Query Agent** – fetches loan-book and hedge positions.
- **Macro-Economic Analysis Agent** – builds scenario ranges and confidence flags.
- **RBAC Agent** – ensures only treasury and strategy teams see the models.

Event 4 – United Bank India Auto-Loan Fraud

- **Loan-SQL Query Agent** – surfaces duplicate chassis numbers and co-owner patterns.
- **Anomaly-Detection Data Agent** – ranks agent IDs by fraud likelihood.
- **Regulatory RAG Agent** – extracts RBI directives for the 90-day show-cause reply.
- **Financial Fraud Compliance Agent** – aligns investigation with RBI customer-protection rules.
- **Legal Action Recommendation Agent** – drafts civil-recovery and criminal pathways.
- **SQL Update Agent** – records findings in the core lending system, black-listing implicated field agents, freezing their accounts, and appending audit notes for future control checks.
- **RBAC Agent** – confines evidence to the fraud unit.
- **Notification Agent** – pushes milestone alerts to country management and counsel.

Disclaimer: *The agent definitions and interactions outlined above are illustrative examples only. Real-world deployments must be designed and validated against an organization's specific governance standards, security controls, and applicable regulatory requirements. Production agents may differ substantially in scope, logic, and safeguards. Use these examples solely as reference material not as definitive blueprints.*

Human Digital Twins: Replicating Human Cognition in AI Applications

Human Digital Twins (HDTs) are advanced digital representations explicitly designed to emulate the cognitive processes, analytical reasoning, and decision-making approaches of human professionals within specialized organizational roles. Unlike typical AI Agents, which manage discrete tasks defined by explicit rules or well-structured logic, Human Digital Twins extend far beyond task execution, incorporating context-specific knowledge, historical memory, and scenario-adaptive reasoning capabilities. This capability allows HDTs to manage complex situations, assess nuanced factors, and formulate robust responses that mirror the analytical depth and deliberate judgment of experienced professionals, enabling organizations to scale expertise reliably.

At their core, Human Digital Twins rely heavily on the precise grounding of knowledge provided by rigorous Data Engineering processes. They draw extensively from structured metadata, explicit regulatory documentation, organizational policies, past case histories, and previously executed scenarios. By systematically leveraging this well-defined foundation of information, Human Digital Twins maintain a persistent, structured memory of past interactions, actions, outcomes, and decisions. This enables HDTs to consistently recognize subtle contextual nuances, effectively replicate the learned wisdom and experience of seasoned professionals, and provide reliably informed, auditable reasoning steps and recommendations in various scenarios.

Unlike human professionals, Human Digital Twins operate strictly within predefined compliant frameworks and organizational governance boundaries, explicitly designed into their architecture. They possess no emotional biases or subjective tendencies, ensuring that recommendations, conclusions, and decisions generated are consistently objective, transparent, and traceable. Each reasoning step, decision rationale, reference to source documentation, and applied regulatory or organizational rule is explicitly logged and made accessible for auditing and accountability purposes. This structured transparency significantly enhances compliance, regulatory oversight, risk management, and organizational control, particularly valuable in sensitive or highly regulated industries such as finance, pharmaceuticals, and healthcare.

In practice, Human Digital Twins collaborate closely with specialized AI Agents, seamlessly interacting with Data Agents to gather accurate, relevant, and timely information from structured databases or unstructured documents. They further leverage Domain Agents for specialized interpretation of regulatory, economic, or industry-specific knowledge. After aggregating insights from these agent interactions, the HDT applies human-like cognitive judgment, synthesizes scenario-specific interpretations, and formulates well-grounded recommendations or decisions. The explicit recording and documentation of every cognitive step ensures complete transparency, accountability, and reproducibility. As a result, enterprises can effectively scale critical expertise across global operations, reduce dependency on limited human resources, maintain consistent quality standards, and ensure ongoing compliance with ever-evolving regulatory demands.

HDT In Action – Payroll Specialist:

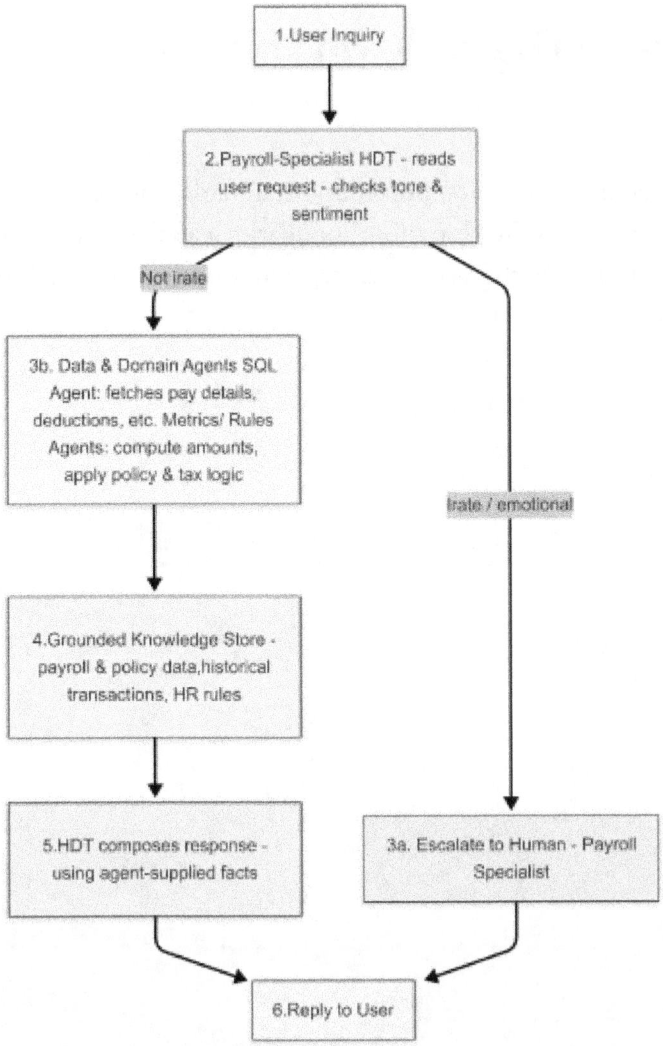

A regulatory-compliance analyst emails Payroll asking why her net pay for April is lower than in March and requests a line-item breakdown of every deduction.

The Payroll-Specialist Human Digital Twin (HDT) receives the message, checks sentiment, and sees the tone is calm not irate so the HDT keeps the case.

The HDT calls the SQL Data Agent, which queries the payroll database for the analyst's April and March pay records, deduction codes, and year-to-date benefit elections.

Next, a Rules/Metric Domain Agent compares the two periods, applies current tax tables and benefit rates from the grounded knowledge store, and tags new or changed items e.g., higher health-insurance premiums that took effect on 1 April.

The agents return structured facts; the HDT assembles a clear explanation: the premium increase plus a catch-up 401(k) contribution account for the exact difference. All figures are linked to authoritative tables for audit.

If the analyst had sounded angry or upset, the HDT would have escalated the email to a human payroll specialist instead of querying the data agents.

Key Characteristics of a Human Digital Twin (HDT)

A Human Digital Twin operates under the organization's established policies, procedural standards, and regulatory obligations, acting as a software counterpart to a specific professional role. Within those boundaries it applies structured reasoning, maintains persistent context, and delivers role-level outputs with traceable transparency qualities that define the essential characteristics explored in the sections that follow.

Has a Specific Role – e.g., Payroll Specialist

A Human Digital Twin is mapped to a clearly bounded professional role. For a payroll specialist, that role spans four core functions:

- **Generate Payroll** calculate each employee's gross pay, commissions, reimbursements, statutory taxes, benefit deductions, and final net pay.
- **Validate Payroll** reconcile aggregate totals, audit tax withholdings, benefit contributions, and ensure regulatory accuracy before funds are released.
- **Onboard and Offboard Employees** establish or deactivate payroll records, banking details, and tax forms as staff join or leave.
- **Address Payroll Inquiries** answer employee pay questions, check sentiment, and route irate cases to a human specialist for personalized managing.

Training an HDT on these role-specific duties guarantees consistent, policy-aligned payroll service with full transparency and auditability.

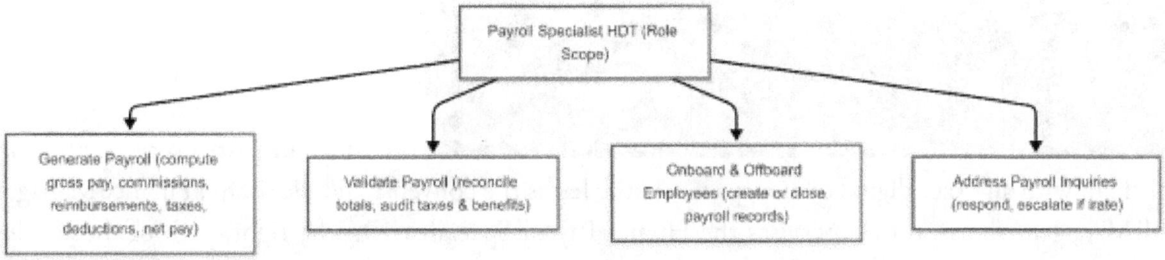

Clear, unambiguous role definition is the cornerstone of every Human Digital Twin. When an HDT's duties are spelled out with precise boundaries such as "compute gross pay, validate deductions, maintain payroll records, answer pay questions" the twin can execute each step confidently and repeatably. Ambiguity invites conflicting instructions, inconsistent outcomes, and audit gaps; precision eliminates those risks by giving the HDT a single source of procedural truth.

Because HDTs have no intrinsic judgement outside their programmed remit, they must never venture beyond the role's written scope. Allowing a payroll twin to alter tax tables, approve expense reports, or share medical data would breach segregation-of-duties rules and expose the organization to financial or regulatory penalties. Strict boundaries preserve compliance, protect sensitive data, and ensure that accountability remains traceable to a well-defined function.

Architects must therefore take great care when crafting the role definition. Every task, data source, exception path, and escalation rule should be documented, peer-reviewed, and approved by domain owners before training begins. Investing time up front guarantees that the HDT remains dependable, auditable, and aligned with organizational controls throughout its lifecycle.

HDTs have Relations:

A Human Digital Twin is embedded in the organization exactly where its human counterpart sits, sharing the same manager, peer group, and escalation paths. By mirroring these existing reporting and collaboration relationships, the twin fits seamlessly into daily operations, is subject to the same oversight, and reinforces rather than alters the company's established workflow and accountability structure.

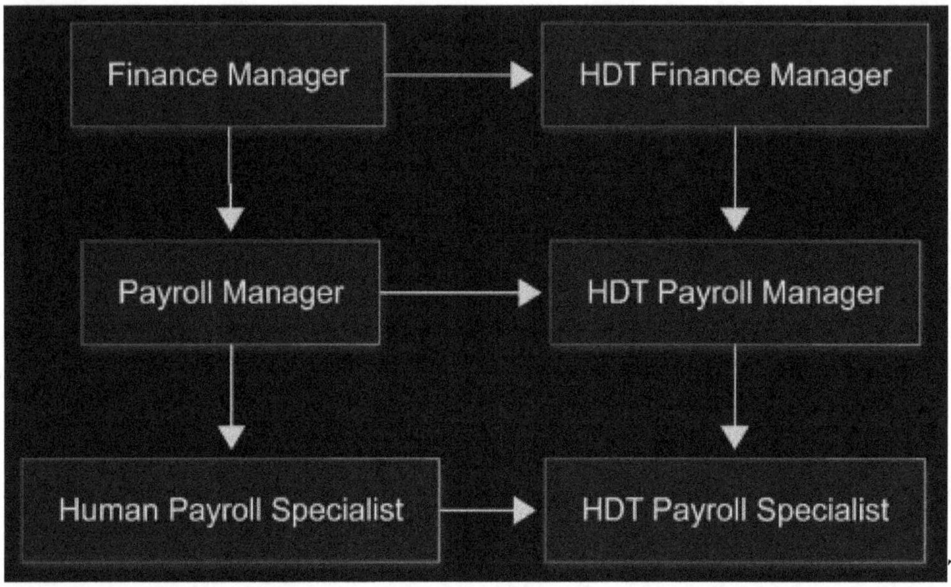

The diagram pairs every position in the finance-payroll chain with an exact digital counterpart. On the left is the conventional hierarchy: Finance Manager oversees the Payroll Manager, who in turn supervises the Human Payroll Specialist. On the right, each of those roles is mirrored by a Human Digital Twin (HDT): an HDT Finance Manager, an HDT Payroll Manager, and an HDT Payroll Specialist. Horizontal arrows indicate one-to-one alignment; each HDT operates at the same authority level and follows the same policies as its human peer. Vertical arrows show that both hierarchies share the identical reporting structure from top to bottom. By duplicating the chain of command in software, the organization preserves existing oversight, escalation paths, and accountability while gaining the speed and consistency benefits delivered by the HDT workforce operating alongside human staff.

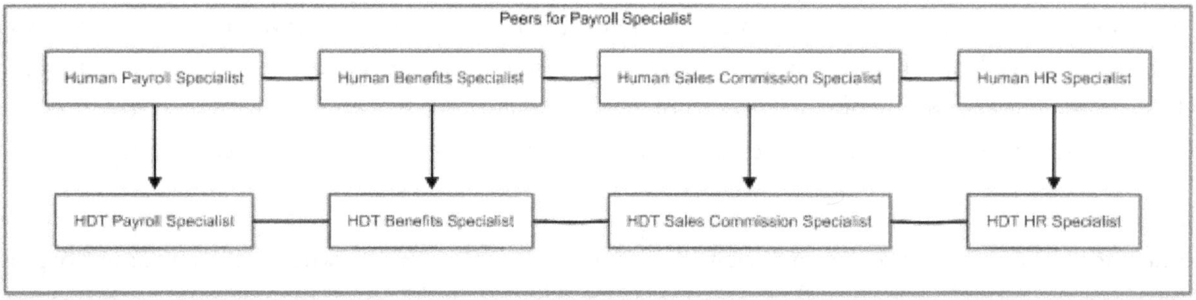

The top row depicts the four human specialists Payroll, Benefits, Sales Commission, and HR joined by horizontal lines that represent their routine collaboration on employee matters. Each expert manages a specific slice of workforce administration but frequently exchanges information with peers when cases overlap.

Directly beneath, the bottom row mirrors this structure with Human Digital Twins for each role. Vertical arrows pair every human with its HDT counterpart, while horizontal links connect the HDTs to one another, replicating the same collaboration pathways. This twin-layer design lets routine, rules-based volume flow to the HDTs while humans focus on exceptions, all within the team framework employees already know.

A payroll inquiry often touches more than pure wage calculations. If an employee's net pay looks off because of a new insurance deduction, the Human Payroll Specialist immediately loops in the Human Benefits Specialist to confirm the premium rate and enrollment date.

The HDT Payroll Specialist follows the same playbook. Detecting that the variance stems from a benefits line, it programmatically asks the HDT Benefits Specialist to validate the deduction against current plan tables. That twin returns a verified figure, allowing the payroll twin to answer the inquiry with full confidence.

By mirroring cross-specialty collaboration, HDTs preserve exactly the same hand-off logic humans rely on. This ensures completeness of information, maintains existing approval chains, and delivers a seamless experience to employees while still reserving complex judgment calls for human peers when necessary.

Embedding the same reporting lines and peer-to-peer channels in the digital workforce is crucial because it keeps governance and accountability unchanged. Managers can oversee HDTs through familiar escalation paths, auditors can trace decisions through the same checkpoints, and employees know exactly where each issue will land whether a human or a twin manages the first response.

Replicating collaboration patterns also maximizes accuracy and trust. When an HDT mirrors the way specialists cross-check each other's work, it prevents gaps that could arise from siloed automation and ensures every answer is vetted by the right domain logic. In short, faithful relationship mapping lets organizations scale expertise with AI while preserving the integrity, compliance, and user confidence already established in human workflows.

HDTs Converse with the Users:

A Human Digital Twin doesn't rush to execute; it begins by conversing. When an employee submits a request, the twin parses the intent and, if details are missing, poses concise follow-up questions much like its human counterpart would in a live call or email thread. Only after the information is complete and unambiguous does the HDT trigger supporting agents or launch downstream workflows. This dialogue-first approach guarantees that every action rests on clear context, prevents costly rework, and preserves the courteous, back-and-forth rhythm employees expect from a skilled specialist.

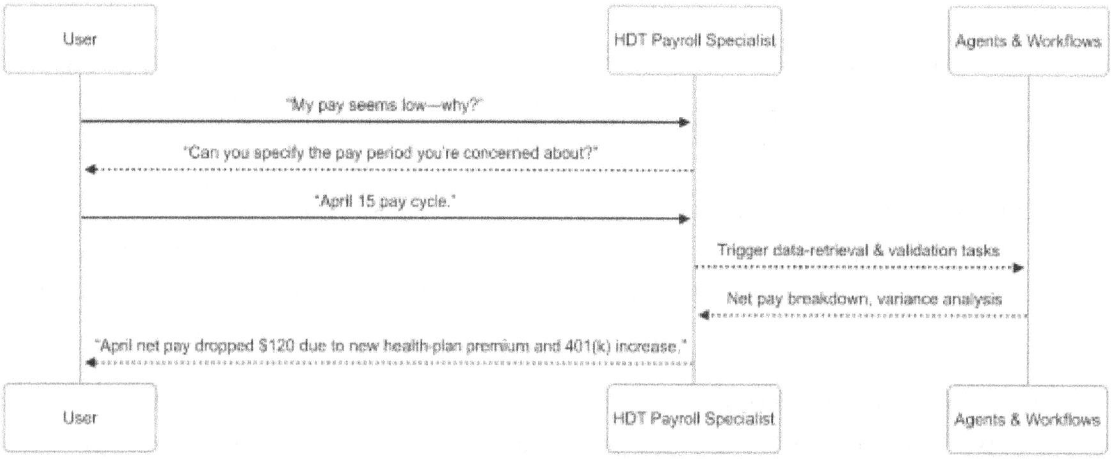

The exchange begins when the employee simply states, "My pay seems low why?" This broad message alerts the HDT Payroll Specialist to a possible discrepancy yet offers no concrete timeframe to investigate, so no data processes are launched at this stage.

Rather than guessing, the HDT asks for a missing detail: "Can you specify the pay period you're concerned about?" Once the employee replies, "April 15 pay cycle," the twin has the precise parameter needed to search the payroll system confidently.

With the period clarified, the HDT triggers its supporting agents to fetch April 15 records, apply policy and tax rules, and compare them with prior cycles. The validated breakdown comes back, and the HDT responds that net pay fell by $120 because of a new health-plan premium and a higher 401(k) contribution, closing the request with a fact-based explanation.

A Human Digital Twin earns its value through dialogue. By asking clarifying questions it gathers the exact context humans normally provide in a back-and-forth chat or email, which prevents wasted processing on vague or incomplete requests. Every interaction also teaches the model subtle patterns in user phrasing, building a richer internal picture of how real employees communicate.

Conversation preserves trust. Users feel heard when the twin mirrors the investigative steps of a live specialist instead of producing a one-shot answer that might miss key details. This exchange lets the HDT confirm identity, learn tone, and recognize when sentiment tips toward frustration so it can hand the case to a person before relations sour.

Dialogue creates audit trails. Each question, reply, and follow-up becomes a logged checkpoint that shows auditors exactly how the twin arrived at its conclusion. That transcript, paired with data pulls and rule checks, satisfies regulators and risk managers who need proof that every pay or benefit explanation rests on documented facts.

In short, careful conversational training is the foundation of a reliable Human Digital Twin, ensuring clarity, user confidence, and full accountability before any automated task starts.

HDTs Provide Reasoning

A Human Digital Twin does not deliver conclusions as opaque black boxes; it explains each step it takes. When the twin compiles an answer, it attaches the rule applied, the data source consulted, and the calculation path followed, so anyone reviewing the exchange can see exactly how the outcome was reached. This built-in reasoning trail mirrors the way a seasoned professional would jot notes and cite references, giving managers, auditors, and users clear visibility into the twin's thought process.

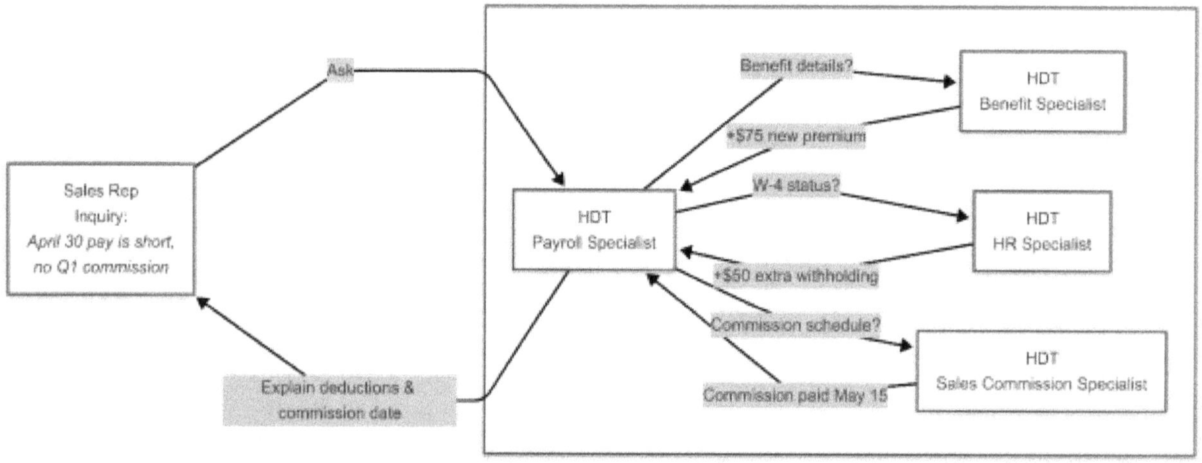

A sales representative reports that her April 30 paycheck is lower than expected and shows no first-quarter commission. The HDT Payroll Specialist receives the message and acknowledges the concern.

The payroll twin checks with the HDT Benefit Specialist, who confirms a $75 health-plan premium increase that took effect in April. It then queries the HDT HR Specialist and learns that the employee filed a new W-4 adding $50 in extra federal withholding.

Next, the twin contacts the HDT Sales Commission Specialist, who verifies that Q1 commissions are scheduled for a separate May 15 payout. With all peer confirmations in hand, the payroll twin compiles the explanation.

It responds to the sales rep, noting that net pay dropped by $125 $75 from the new premium and $50 from the updated withholding and that the Q1 commission will appear on the May 15 paycheck.

Employees accept an automated response only when they see how the conclusion was reached. By citing each data source the premium update from Benefits, the W-4 change from HR, the commission schedule from Sales Compensation the HDT shows that its answer rests on verifiable facts, not guesswork. Transparent reasoning builds immediate credibility.

Detailed explanation also lets auditors trace the path from inquiry to resolution. Every peer confirmation is logged, so compliance officers can verify that payroll, benefits, and tax rules were applied exactly as policy requires. This audit trail shields the company from disputes and regulatory questions.

Most important, clear reasoning respects the employee's need for understanding. When the sales rep learns precisely why net pay changed and when commission will post, frustration turns to confidence. In short, explicit explanations turn an HDT from a black box into a trusted digital colleague.

HDTs know which agents to invoke and when

A well-designed Human Digital Twin does more than mirror human judgment; it serves as the intelligent switchboard that routes work to the exact specialists Data, Domain, or Utility agents needed for each task. The twin interprets a user's request, identifies the data gaps or rule checks involved, and selectively triggers only those agents that can supply the missing pieces. By orchestrating this targeted collaboration, the HDT ensures every response is grounded in authoritative sources, delivered efficiently, and aligned with organizational policy without burdening the system with unnecessary processing.

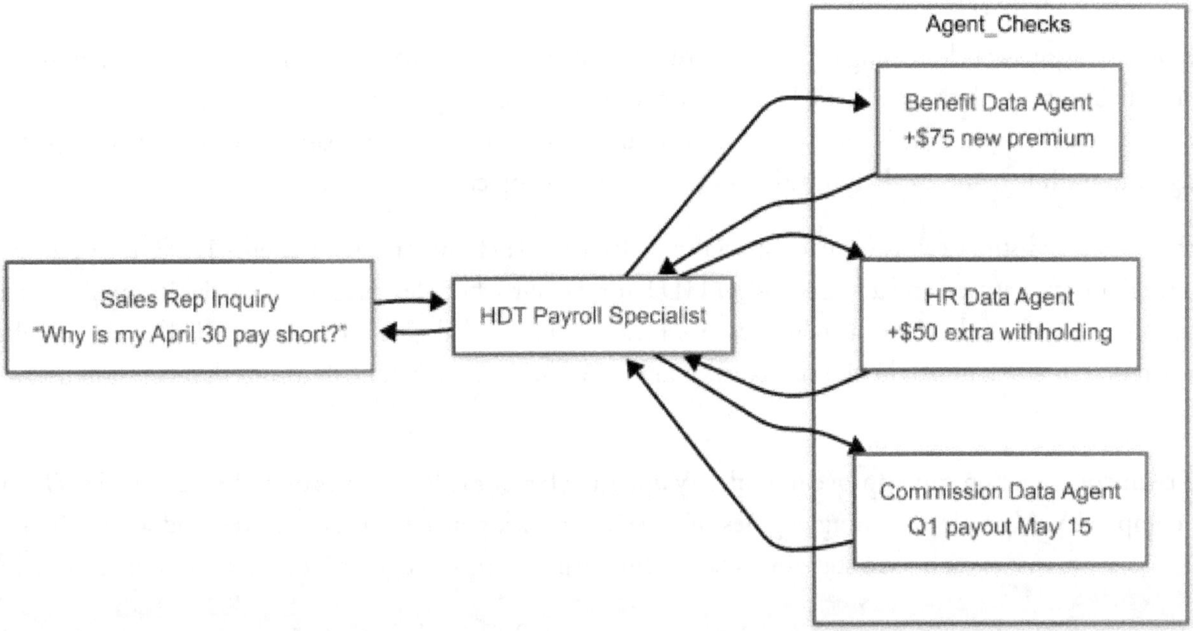

The diagram begins with the sales representative's simple question "Why is my April 30 pay short?" entering the HDT Payroll Specialist. Before doing anything else, the twin parses the request, confirms the employee's identity, and notes that the concern centers on a specific pay cycle. Rather than launching a blind calculation, the HDT first identifies which data domains can explain net-pay variance and then dispatches targeted requests.

It contacts the Benefit Data Agent to see if recent benefit elections or premium changes might have increased deductions. That agent queries the benefits ledger and reports a $75 rise in the employee's health-plan premium that started with the April run. Next, the HDT asks the HR Data Agent to verify any tax-withholding or employment-status changes. HR responds that the employee filed a new W-4 earlier in the month, adding an extra $50 of federal withholding. Finally, the HDT consults the Commission Data Agent because sales personnel often have variable earnings. That agent checks the commission-management system and confirms that first-quarter commissions are scheduled for a separate May 15 payment, so none appeared in the April 30 cycle.

With all three facts returned, the HDT integrates them into a concise, traceable answer. It calculates the net-pay drop ($75 premium plus $50 withholding = $125) and assures the sales rep that the missing Q1 commission will post on May 15. By sourcing each component from the authoritative system of record and citing them in the reply, the twin provides both clarity and audit-ready evidence mirroring the diligence a seasoned payroll professional would apply, but in seconds instead of hours.

Invoking the correct agent is vital because each agent encapsulates a narrow, certified slice of knowledge. When the HDT Payroll Specialist selects the Benefits, HR, and Commission agents, it guarantees that data come from systems of record managed by their respective owners. If the twin chose the wrong source or skipped an agent entirely the response could omit a deduction, double-count a benefit, or misstate a commission schedule, eroding employee trust and exposing the company to payroll-compliance risk.

Correct targeting also preserves traceability. By logging which agent supplied each figure, the HDT can reproduce every step if auditors question a paycheck. A clean hand-off chain from twin to agent to source system creates an end-to-end audit trail; any deviation breaks that chain and undermines accountability.

Architecturally, organizations can let a single HDT coordinate all supporting agents, or they can build hierarchies where one HDT collaborates with other HDTs. In the first pattern seen in the payroll example the Payroll Twin alone orchestrates every data call. Its reasoning is centralized, and all supporting agents remain passive helpers. This simplicity eases monitoring: one audit log, one escalation path, one place to refine logic.

The second pattern assigns distinct twins for each specialty. A Payroll HDT might ask a Benefits HDT for premium details, an HR HDT for tax statuses, and a Commission HDT for payout schedules. Each twin carries its own context, memory, and reasoning rules. Orchestration then becomes HDT-to-HDT dialogue rather than HDT-to-agent calls. This mirrors human practice even more closely: specialists confer peer-to-peer, each contributing judgment, not just raw data.

Such role-based twin collaboration can improve modularity updating benefit rules touches only the Benefits HDT but it raises design complexity. Multiple reasoning engines must synchronize, manage partial failures, and avoid circular queries. Governance must ensure each twin stays in its lane while still sharing enough context to answer cross-domain questions.

Determining which pattern to use is an architectural decision, not something to bolt on later in implementation. The choice affects data-flow design, security boundaries, audit strategy, and performance budgets; shifting patterns mid-build forces costly re-engineering of interfaces, logs, and compliance controls. Architects must weigh data volumes, team skills, maintenance overhead, and regulatory expectations before locking in the coordination model.

At architecture time, designers also decide escalation paths, credential scopes, and monitoring dashboards. These elements differ sharply between single-twin orchestration and multi-twin collaboration. Leaving the decision to implementation risks mismatched logs, duplicated logic, and unclear ownership when production issues arise.

A single-twin model offers simplicity and fewer moving parts but can grow monolithic and harder to maintain. Multi-twin collaboration mirrors human divisions of labor, boosts modularity, and eases domain updates, yet increases orchestration complexity and coordination overhead.

Whatever pattern is chosen, the guiding principle is consistent: clear boundaries, explicit hand-offs, and auditable reasoning. A well-defined architecture ensures every HDT knows exactly when and whether to call an agent or a fellow twin, delivering reliable answers that stand up to scrutiny.

HDTs Escalate Issues to Human Specialists and HDT Line Managers

Human Digital Twins excel at rule application but lack true empathy. Deterministic logic, historical data, and policy tables drive every action, leaving no space for authentic feelings or real-time social cues. Subtle signals such as frustration in a user's tone often elude algorithmic interpretation, even with advanced sentiment analysis.

Emotional nuance matters when pay affects livelihood or benefits touch family well-being. Misreading a distressed employee risks compounding anxiety and damaging trust. Escalation to a human specialist allows genuine listening, apologies when appropriate, and adaptive phrasing that resonates with the individual's state of mind.

Situational judgment presents another gap. Edge-case scenarios retroactive pay changes after a legal settlement, overlapping leave policies, or culturally sensitive deductions require discretionary reasoning no fixed policy tree can fully encode. A trained human weighs precedent, equity, and evolving regulations before making adjustments that stand up to scrutiny.

Escalation paths address these limits. The HDT monitors language and context for predefined emotional and situational triggers. Exceeding those thresholds prompts an immediate hand-off to a human payroll specialist who can intervene with empathy and holistic insight.

Not every complication demands frontline human involvement; some belong to the next tier in the digital hierarchy. An HDT Payroll Manager twin oversees broader policy intersections and carries higher authority. When a case involves multi-department rules yet remains fundamentally procedural, the primary twin forwards it to its managerial counterpart for resolution.

Line-manager twins also smooth workload spikes. High inquiry volumes can strain a single HDT, so the managerial twin redistributes tasks to peer twins or schedules follow-up calls with human teams. This keeps service levels steady without overwhelming any one resource.

Governance escalations follow the same ladder. Metadata gaps, conflicting database entries, or potential fraud indicators trigger alerts to the line-manager twin. That twin either initiates higher-privilege data agents for correction or routes the case directly to compliance officers for rapid human oversight.

Clear escalation design maintains accountability and transparency. Logs show exactly when the HDT recognized its boundaries, who assumed responsibility, and which rules guided each step. Automation thus operates within human-centric safeguards, marrying efficiency with empathy and robust organizational control.

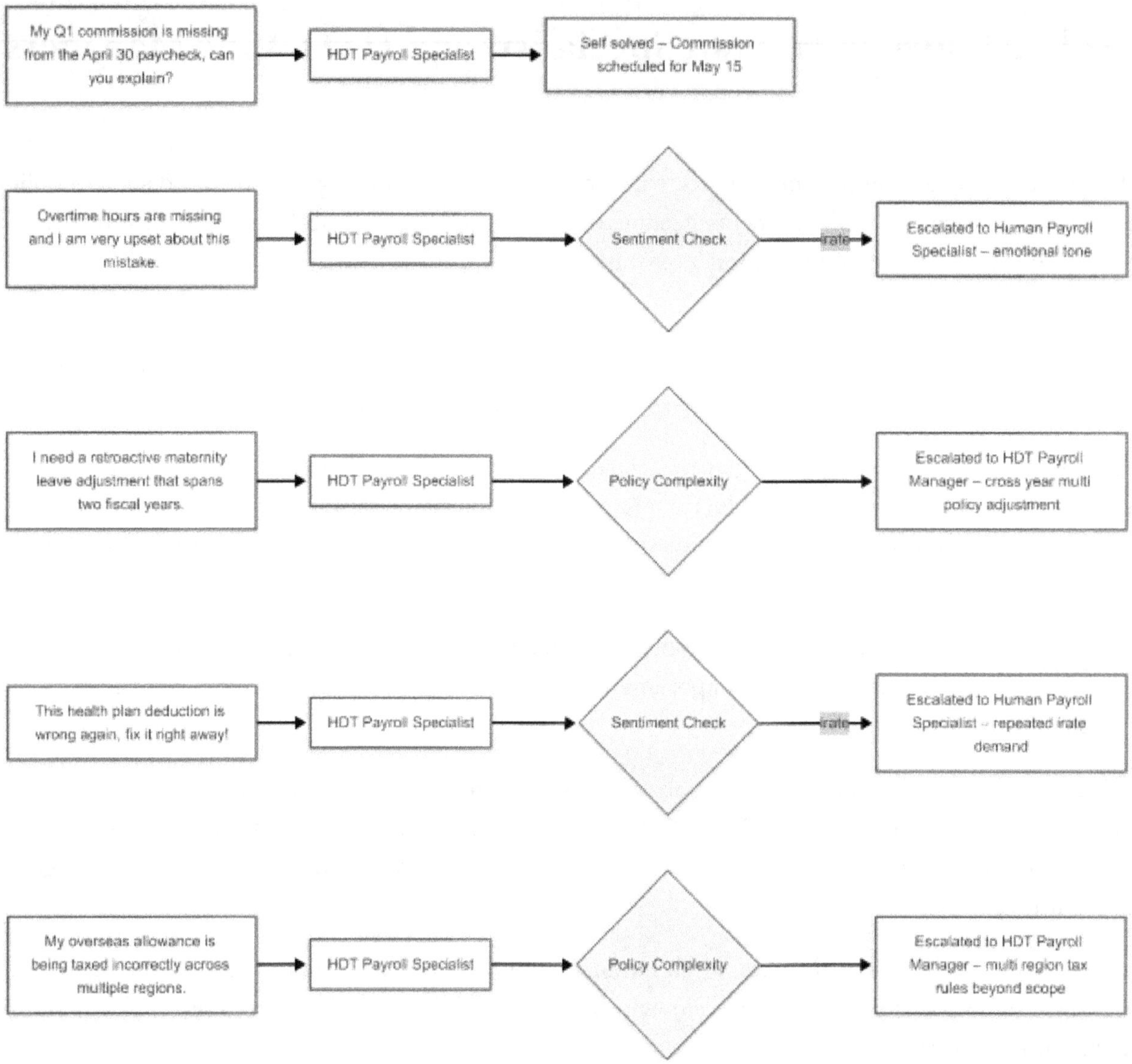

The first employee asks why Q1 commission is absent from the April 30 paycheck. The HDT Payroll Specialist checks the commission schedule in the sales-compensation database, confirms that Q1 payouts are processed on the May 15 off-cycle run, and validates the entry in the grounded knowledge store. With clear data and no sentiment concerns or policy conflicts, the twin can answer directly, so it self-solves and informs the employee that payment will appear on May 15.

In the second case an employee complains loudly that overtime hours are missing. Sentiment analysis flags the wording as irate, crossing the HDT's escalation threshold set for emotionally charged language. To avoid further frustration and to provide empathetic interaction, the twin immediately passes the inquiry to a human payroll specialist who can address the concern in a conversational, reassuring manner while also investigating the overtime discrepancy.

The third inquiry requests a retroactive maternity-leave adjustment spanning two fiscal years. The HDT recognizes that multiple policy documents leave regulations, tax year boundaries, and cross-year benefit corrections must be reconciled. Marked as policy complexity, this exceeds the twin's authority and rule set. Consequently, the HDT escalates to its line-manager twin, the HDT Payroll Manager, which holds broader policy logic and can coordinate with HR and finance to perform the adjustment properly.

For the fourth request an employee demands immediate correction of a health-plan deduction error, using aggressive language. Sentiment analysis again detects an irate tone, triggering escalation to a human payroll specialist. The HDT transfers the case so a person can apologize, defuse tension, and investigate whether the deduction issue stems from benefits enrollment or system error.

The fifth inquiry concerns overseas allowance taxation across multiple regions. The HDT identifies conflicting jurisdictional tax rules and notes that resolution requires higher-level authority and multi-region policy alignment. Labeled as policy complexity, the case is routed to the HDT Payroll Manager twin, which can access international tax guidelines and coordinate with the global mobility team to correct withholding and document compliance.

Human Digital Twins must know when a situation exceeds their scripted boundaries, otherwise they risk offering incomplete or incorrect answers that erode employee confidence. Escalation training draws a bright line: the twin handles routine, rule-based cases, but steps aside when sentiment or policy complexity signals that human discretion is required. This discipline mirrors the judgment calls human specialists make every day.

Clear escalation thresholds keep the twin from guessing. If an inquiry references multiple tax years or crosses regulatory jurisdictions, the HDT recognizes that its rule set may not account for every nuance. By routing the matter upward or outward, the twin preserves accuracy and avoids opaque "best-effort" replies that could later be challenged in audits.

Sentiment detection is equally important. An agitated or anxious employee expects empathy, not boilerplate text. Training the HDT to spot tone markers words, punctuation, even typing rhythm helps it decide whether to continue autonomously or transfer the conversation to a human who can defuse tension and build rapport.

Policy complexity triggers a different hand-off. Leave calculations spanning fiscal years, cross-border tax questions, or unique benefit arrangements often require multi-department coordination. The HDT's escalation logic sends such cases to an HDT line manager or a designated human team that owns wider authority, ensuring that approvals and checks stay within governance boundaries.

Effective routing also relies on the twin's knowledge of specialist agents. When the HDT calls Benefits, HR, or Commission agents, it must track which data each can supply and in what format. Well defined routing ensures the twin pulls correct figures from systems of record instead of defaulting to generic estimates preventing hallucinated numbers that undermine trust.

Training these behaviors forces designers to codify business rules, escalation paths, and agent capabilities in explicit metadata. Large language models consume that metadata and learn exactly which steps to take, reducing the temptation to generate authoritative-sounding but unverified content. Detailed routing logic therefore acts as a guardrail against hallucination.

Escalation transparency also satisfies audit and compliance demands. Logs show when the HDT recognized a boundary, which agent or person took over, and what facts supported the final decision. Regulators and internal auditors can trace every hand-off, verifying that automation never overrides human oversight in sensitive cases.

In short, teaching an HDT when and how to escalate is as critical as training it to answer. Defined thresholds, sentiment checks, and agent routing keep responses accurate, auditable, and respectful of human context, while preventing large language models from venturing beyond safe limits. Proper escalation design secures both technical reliability and organizational trust.

What Tasks Should HDTs Perform And Which Ones Should They Avoid?

The overarching goal of implementing any technology, software, or process including AI, and specifically Human Digital Twins (HDTs) is to achieve measurable efficiency gains that deliver clear monetary and non-monetary value to the organization. For this reason, careful thought must go into determining which tasks HDTs should perform and which tasks must remain firmly within human oversight. Activities and processes positioned on an organization's critical path those whose mismanagement or failure could result in significant financial risk, damage employee morale, or negatively affect public perception should never be assigned entirely to HDTs. The rationale is straightforward: tasks involving payroll calculation, sales commission payments, and similarly sensitive areas directly impact employees' livelihoods and organizational trust. A payroll error, for instance, quickly translates into dissatisfaction, loss of employee confidence, and even external reputational harm, creating a lasting negative impact.

The restriction of critical-path activities to human personnel is not a limitation unique to HDTs. Even existing technologies, such as Robotic Process Automation (RPA) and Machine Learning (ML), are deliberately kept clear of core payroll execution or commission calculations precisely because of the inherent risks. Despite their advanced capabilities, these technologies like HDTs can occasionally produce unforeseen errors or inaccuracies. Therefore, any activity that, if mishandled, would directly and negatively impact the organization's stability or employees' morale should remain exclusively under human accountability.

Nevertheless, many essential activities fall outside the strict boundaries of the critical path yet are integral components of broader operational processes. These are best categorized as quality or complementary activities supportive tasks that ensure the smooth execution of primary functions. Consider payroll processing: before any payroll run, significant human effort is dedicated to preliminary quality checks. Tasks such as verifying the accuracy of new employee information, confirming that terminated employees have been properly offboarded, or validating whether all necessary payroll approvals have been obtained consume substantial resources. Similar scenarios occur in commission calculations, where extensive data validation and accuracy checks precede the core calculation, or in financial audits, where preparatory reconciliations and documentation validations precede audit reviews.

In the context of payroll, a human payroll specialist rightly retains responsibility for executing the final payroll run, ensuring all employees are paid accurately and on schedule. The specialist also remains responsible for sensitive transactions such as entering or removing employees from payroll systems and directly authorizing payroll changes. On the other hand, HDTs offer significant value in performing meticulous pre-run validations such as checking if deductions have been properly established for new employees, verifying completed approval chains, or identifying terminated employees whose payroll status remains active. Further, HDTs can validate whether salary adjustments conform to policy, confirm overtime calculations, or flag discrepancies in tax withholding. Each of these supportive activities currently demands significant manual labor, is highly repetitive, and yet is crucial for organizational accuracy and compliance.

In addition to pre-processing tasks, HDTs can considerably reduce the burden of administrative follow-up. For example, after payroll is finalized, the HDT can automatically compile the necessary payroll slides and supporting documentation required for monthly review meetings. The human payroll manager then only needs to verify and validate the accuracy of these reports rather than manually prepare them, thereby redirecting their efforts toward strategic analysis and decision-making in collaboration with the human finance manager. This division of labor ensures humans continue managing critical tasks while the HDTs manage repetitive yet essential preparatory work, maintaining the integrity of organizational processes.

By taking responsibility for these meticulous quality-check and complementary activities, HDTs significantly reduce the workload of human personnel without compromising the rigor required in sensitive organizational functions. The tangible result is a reduction in errors, improvements in process speed, increased organizational efficiency, and heightened employee satisfaction due to fewer disruptions and greater payroll accuracy. Organizations can thus redirect valuable human expertise toward higher-level tasks, strategic planning, and exception management, optimizing the value derived from both human and digital resources.

Ultimately, the judicious deployment of HDTs alongside human specialists, with clearly defined roles and boundaries, offers organizations the potential to achieve measurable operational improvements. While HDTs manage the necessary, routine validation tasks, humans remain fully accountable for core activities, thereby achieving efficiency, accuracy, and reliability without sacrificing employee trust, morale, or organizational reputation.

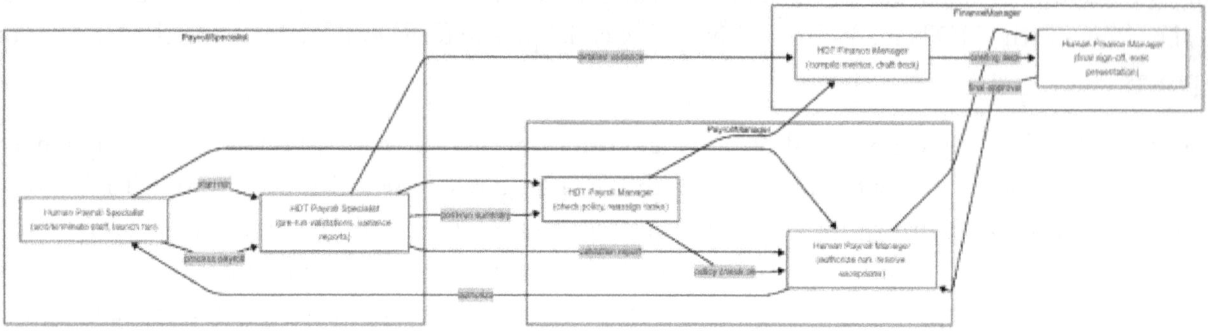

At the left edge, the employee-facing work starts with the Human Payroll Specialist. That person carries authority to modify the payroll ledger, add or terminate employees, and press the button that initiates the monthly processing routine. Once that launch order is issued, the instruction flows horizontally to the HDT Payroll Specialist. The digital twin immediately runs a battery of checks: every current worker must have a valid deduction set, any employee terminated after the prior cycle must be absent from active registers, overtime entries must match time-clock data, and approval signatures must appear for salary changes. Findings are consolidated into a validation report and sent forward to the Human Payroll Manager.

The Human Payroll Manager reviews the HDT's findings. When nothing critical is missing the manager returns an authorization signal to the human specialist, allowing the live payroll run to proceed. After the run completes, confirmation travels back to the HDT Payroll Specialist so the twin can capture post-run details gross pay totals, withholding figures, and per-employee variances from the prior month. Those summary numbers move upward inside the digital hierarchy to the HDT Payroll Manager.

Within the center band the HDT Payroll Manager compares the HDT specialist's post-run summaries to corporate policy thresholds. It looks for items such as unusually high bonus payouts or abrupt shifts in benefit costs. If everything aligns with policy, the digital manager sends a policy-check-OK message to the Human Payroll Manager, closing the loop on compliance. Should exceptions surface, the same path would carry detailed alerts instead, prompting human review and possible correction before financial close.

On the right side the information climbs toward finance leadership. The HDT Payroll Specialist also directs a detailed variance file to the HDT Finance Manager. That file contains line-item deltas by cost center, tax authority totals, and benefit accrual movements. The HDT Finance Manager converts the raw numbers into executive-ready charts and narrative commentary, then forwards a briefing deck to the Human Finance Manager.

With the briefing in hand, the Human Finance Manager evaluates year-to-date trend lines, spot-checks any anomalies flagged by the HDTs, and ultimately signs off on the cycle. Final approval flows back to the Human Payroll Manager, signaling closure for the month and authorizing distribution of reports to senior leadership. Throughout the entire sequence, humans manage the decisions that carry financial or reputational weight, while HDTs perform every repetitive, detail-heavy check and compilation step. Logs of each hand-off reveal exactly when the digital twins acted, what they checked, and the moment responsibility shifted to a human, ensuring clear auditability and sustained trust in the combined human–digital process.

Determining Task Ownership Between Humans and HDTs

Criticality of Outcome:

Tasks with substantial organizational consequences such as payroll calculation, sales commission distribution, or compliance reporting should remain with human specialists to maintain direct accountability. Conversely, HDTs are suitable for supporting roles like verifying preliminary information or preparing routine documentation.

Emotional and Situational Judgment Required:

Activities involving nuanced emotional interactions or complex situational decision-making, such as employee grievance managing or interpreting sensitive employee circumstances, must remain under human control. HDTs, lacking inherent empathy, are best suited for standard procedural workflows.

Regulatory Compliance and Legal Risks:

Processes entailing legal scrutiny or regulatory oversight, such as financial disclosures, taxation compliance, or benefit elections, should primarily be human-owned, with HDTs supporting through meticulous documentation and validation rather than direct execution.

Frequency and Repetition:

Highly repetitive and frequent tasks validating deductions, checking policy adherence, or summarizing routine variances can be effectively managed by HDTs, freeing human experts for tasks requiring advanced analysis or discretionary decisions.

Complexity of Cross-Departmental Coordination:

If tasks require extensive collaboration across multiple departments or policy domains such as retroactive payroll adjustments spanning multiple fiscal periods initial assessments and routine verifications can be delegated to HDTs, but final approvals and exceptions should remain human-driven.

Sensitivity of Data Involved:

Tasks involving sensitive personal or financial information, such as salary adjustments or confidential medical leave details, must include human oversight to ensure adherence to privacy standards. HDTs can assist in preliminary verification, but final managing and decision-making remain human responsibilities.

Auditability and Traceability:

Tasks that require robust audit trails and transparent traceability, such as payroll processing or financial reconciliations, benefit greatly from HDT involvement for documentation and validation. However, authoritative approvals and accountability for final results should continue to be human-driven to satisfy regulatory and auditing bodies.

Impact on Employee Trust and Morale:

Activities directly influencing employee compensation, career, or workplace well-being such as pay determinations, bonus allocations, or sensitive communications must remain human-led. HDTs can support these areas by managing preliminary processes to improve accuracy, but humans retain ultimate control to sustain organizational trust.

Considering these factors helps organizations achieve a balanced and effective division of responsibilities, maximizing efficiency while safeguarding accuracy, compliance, and trust.

Determining which tasks remain human-owned and which tasks are delegated to HDTs must be finalized at the architecture stage, prior to initiating any development. At the architectural level, critical considerations such as organizational accountability, regulatory compliance, and employee trust can be thoroughly analyzed, enabling a robust design. Attempting to resolve these factors later, after technical development has started, risks introducing costly revisions, conflicting workflows, or security vulnerabilities that could undermine the project's success.

When task ownership clarity is established upfront, architects can explicitly define the interaction boundaries, ensuring human roles are clear and HDT responsibilities align precisely with organizational policies. Clearly delineated boundaries minimize the risk of duplication, confusion, and compliance violations, creating transparency around accountability and enhancing organizational trust. Early determination also allows architects to implement accurate logging and audit trails, essential for maintaining regulatory compliance and enabling traceability from initiation to resolution.

Postponing task allocation decisions until the implementation phase often leads to expensive rework and potential misalignment between human and digital roles. It can also introduce ambiguity into the system's logic, increasing the chance that AI models or HDTs misinterpret their intended scope, resulting in inaccuracies or compliance risks. A structured, early-stage allocation ensures clear, well-understood processes, reducing ambiguity for developers, data engineers, and quality assurance teams, and avoiding costly corrective actions later in the implementation.

In conclusion, performing a detailed task ownership exercise at the architecture stage ensures alignment between business objectives, human oversight, and technical execution. It sets the foundation for a trustworthy and transparent operational environment, optimizing the complementary capabilities of human specialists and HDTs. Ultimately, this upfront investment in careful planning provides long-term operational stability, clarity, and compliance, enhancing the effectiveness and value derived from HDT initiatives.

HDT Structure

HDT_Template:

name: "<HDT_Unique_Name>" # (AI-readable) Provide a distinctive, stable identifier that the language model can reference when resolving interaction contexts, ensuring unambiguous linkage between this twin and all downstream agent exchanges, peer calls, and reporting paths.

role_description: |

"<Insert a role narrative no shorter than 250 characters. Describe professional objectives, essential domain knowledge, required policy familiarity, and the HDT's responsibility boundaries. This extended text gives the LLM enough surface area to build an accurate internal representation of authority, expected outputs, and compliance thresholds.>"

scope_of_work: |

"<Detail every task assigned to the twin in 250+ characters. Enumerate routine validations, data lookups, pre-checks, report generation, follow-up steps, and any automated communications. Lengthy scope text guides the LLM to recognize permissible actions and prevents it from hallucinating unauthorized behaviors.>"

out_of_scope: |

"<Specify tasks strictly prohibited for the twin, again using at least 250 characters. Clarify that salary calculations, final approvals, or emotionally nuanced conversations require human specialists. The LLM will use this to block requests that exceed role limits and to trigger escalation logic.>"

system_access:

allowed_systems: # (AI-readable) Each entry explains to the LLM which endpoints it may query.

- system_name: "<Database_or_API>"

credentials_reference: "<Vault_Path_or_Token_Handle>"

access_level: "<ReadOnly_or_Writable>"

usage_description: |

"<Minimum 250-character explanation of how this HDT employs the system, including query patterns, data filters, and why the connection is necessary for accurate performance.>"

reporting_workflow:

manager: "<Parent_Human_or_HDT_Manager_ID>" # (AI-readable) Guides escalation routing.

escalation_conditions: |

"<Describe, in 250+ characters, the exact conditions that prompt the twin to route an issue to its manager sentiment thresholds, policy conflicts, or data anomalies so the LLM knows when to hand off.>"

audit_logging: |

"<Detail the logging schema used to capture each action, ensuring traceability. Minimum 250 characters so the language model fully understands how and where to store reasoning trails, timestamps, and source references.>"

interactions:

agent_calls:

- agent_name: "<Supporting_Agent_ID>"

trigger_conditions: |

"<At least 250 characters describing when the HDT invokes this agent, what parameters it passes, and how the response is consumed. This precise guidance prevents the LLM from calling irrelevant agents.>"

peer_collaboration:

- peer_name: "<Human_or_HDT_Peer_ID>"

collaboration_flow: |

"<Explain collaboration steps in no fewer than 250 characters information exchange cadence, mutual validations, conflict resolution, and context sharing so the LLM can replicate established teamwork patterns accurately.>"

version_control:

version: "<Semantic_Version_Number>"

last_update: "<YYYY-MM-DD>"

change_log: |

"<Provide a history entry (≥250 characters) explaining what changed in this version new agent endpoints, updated escalation rules, revised policy references allowing the LLM to maintain backward compatibility and explain reasoning shifts.>"

HDT Payroll Specialist

HDT_Profile:

The LLM reads the "name" field first, uses it as a unique anchor to map user requests

or system events to this specific twin, and avoids confusing it with other payroll or

benefits twins in memory.

name: "HDT_Payroll_Specialist"

role_description: |

"This Human Digital Twin emulates the full reasoning flow of a tenured payroll specialist who supports bi-weekly and monthly cycles across multiple tax jurisdictions and benefit plans. It maintains persistent memory of pay schedules, benefit deduction logic, union contract clauses, garnishment rules, and multi-state tax tables. The twin validates upstream data feeds, spots anomalies such as inactive direct-deposit accounts, and documents every decision with source citations. Because this paragraph exceeds 250 characters, the LLM parses it into multiple semantic chunks duties, authority scope, and compliance obligations helping it avoid hallucinations about tasks or data access that lie outside the stated boundaries."

The length and specificity give the model a rich mental schema of responsibilities,

enabling accurate reasoning and proper escalation behavior.

scope_of_work: |

"The twin performs exhaustive pre-run validations: checking new-hire deduction setups, confirming that terminated employees are inactive, verifying supervisor-approved overtime batches, and scanning bank routing numbers for validity. It also compares current gross pay, commissions, reimbursements, taxes, and deductions with prior cycles, flagging deviations beyond policy tolerance. After payroll executes, it assembles variance reports and ledger extracts for finance. By providing more than 250 characters, the LLM gains detailed procedural steps to follow, which keeps it from skipping validations or inventing new ones."

The LLM uses these details as a checklist, ensuring it does not attempt the live payroll

run itself but focuses on validation and reporting only.

out_of_scope: |

"Executing live payroll runs, approving salary adjustments, overriding tax tables, changing deduction codes, or conducting sensitive terminations are strictly off-limits. Situations that involve multi-year retroactive pay, wage garnishment disputes, or suspected fraud must be escalated. The extended length supplies the LLM with explicit red lines; any user prompt touching these areas triggers refusal or escalation instead of improvisation."

This block instructs the model to reject or transfer any request that crosses these limits,

reducing risk of unauthorized actions.

system_access:

allowed_systems:

- system_name: "Payroll_DB_ReadReplica"

credentials_reference: "Vault/Payroll/ReadOnlyToken"

access_level: "ReadOnly"

usage_description: |

"Queries fetch employee master data, earnings history, deduction tables, and reconciliation flags via parameterized SQL keyed by employee ID, period, and cost center. Results feed integrity scripts, then are SHA-256 hashed for audit. The language model interprets this as a read-only endpoint; any attempt to write or delete records violates role policy and triggers an automatic refusal."

Comment: The LLM treats this description as an execution blueprint only READ queries

with strict filters are valid; write operations are blocked.

- system_name: "Timekeeping_API"

credentials_reference: "Vault/Timekeeping/OAuth"

access_level: "ReadOnly"

usage_description: |

"The twin retrieves approved overtime hours and shift differentials, correlating them with payroll cut-off dates. Any overtime lacking supervisor sign-off is flagged. By detailing query filters, rate conversions, and reconciliation steps in over 250 characters, the LLM learns exactly what data to fetch and how to integrate it without surfacing unrelated employee information."

Comment: Guides the model to pull only scoped fields; extraneous calls become invalid.

reporting_workflow:

manager: "Human_Payroll_Manager" # The LLM routes escalations here by default.

escalation_conditions: |

"Escalate when missing bank details exceed three percent of active employees, when deduction codes mismatch benefit enrollments, when sentiment analysis flags irate language, or when cross-border tax logic requires discretionary decisions. The lengthy text equips the LLM with precise thresholds and triggers so it does not hesitate or second-guess escalation rules."

audit_logging: |

"Every SQL query, API call, reasoning summary, and escalation packet is time-stamped in UTC and stored in the Payroll_Audit_Log table, mirrored to encrypted S3 storage. Hashes of raw results ensure tamper detection. The LLM interprets this as a mandate to produce exhaustive logs for each step, supporting post-event audits and compliance reviews."

Comment: The model uses these instructions to guarantee traceability in every action.

interactions:

agent_calls:

- agent_name: "Benefit_Data_Agent"

trigger_conditions: |

"Called whenever deduction code changes, premium rate updates, or new benefit enrollments occur in the current pay period. Employee IDs and plan codes are passed in a structured JSON payload. A ≥250-character narrative teaches the LLM the precise scenario for invocation and prevents unnecessary or duplicate calls."

Comment: Helps the model avoid unneeded agent interactions, saving compute budget.

peer_collaboration:

- peer_name: "HDT_Benefit_Specialist"

collaboration_flow: |

"When benefit variances exceed policy thresholds, the Payroll twin sends a request containing plan IDs, variance percentages, and employee counts. The Benefits twin returns verified rate tables and approval references. The detailed flow instructs the LLM on data sharing cadence, ensuring privacy compliance while allowing accurate fact-checking."

Comment: The model follows this pattern to maintain secure, role-appropriate data exchange.

version_control:

version: "1.0.0"

last_update: "2025-04-20"

change_log: |

"Initial version introduces validation logic for deductions, taxes, and bank routing; integrates Benefit_Data_Agent; defines escalation thresholds for irate language and multi-jurisdiction tax challenges; implements SHA-256 audit hashing. Over 250 characters ensure the LLM can reconcile historical reasoning differences between versions and provide backward-compatible explanations."

Comment: The versioning narrative helps the model explain behavior changes when queried.

Event Example – Human and HDT Actions

Event 1 Fast Legs Contract-Performance Analysis

Human actions

Approve the final six-quarter performance slide before it reaches the board.

Interpret any ambiguous contract language or board follow-up questions.

Sign off on the 340B versus non-340B figures after reviewing HRSA validation output.

HDT actions

Extract shipment, unit, and net-sales data from SAP and the data warehouse.

Validate every 340B transaction date against the HRSA Covered-Entity list.

Pull contract PDF clauses with a RAG agent and summarize five key terms.

Generate the rolling-quarter tables, variance calculations, and single-sentence peer comparison; assemble the draft board slide.

Event 2 Bioncology Principal-Investigator Fraud

Human actions

Interview internal study teams, decide on PI suspension, and coordinate ethics-committee notifications.

Authorize mandatory FDA and EMA disclosures and oversee external communications.

Review and approve blacklist entries before they take effect in vendor and CRM systems.

HDT actions

Scrape trial registry records and document timelines of the investigator's involvement.

Search contract repositories for PI agreements and extract non-compliance clauses.

Populate a remediation checklist covering data-lock, re-consent, and audit-trail preservation steps.

Write database updates that flag the PI as blacklisted and remove KOL status, pending human approval.

Event 3 United Bank Interest-Rate Scenario

Human actions

Validate economic assumptions and adjust scenario probabilities.

Present the rate-cut impact slide deck to the board and answer questions on strategic funding moves.

Approve any treasury-hedging transactions that follow the board meeting.

HDT actions

Collect analyst reports, central-bank minutes, and news feeds, ranking them by source credibility and recency.

Run SQL queries on the bank's loan-book and swap ledger to quantify earnings sensitivity at each basis-point cut.

Compile a consolidated timeline showing expected effective dates and cumulative rate-cut totals.

Draft a one-page board summary with graphs and confidence indicators for human economist review.

Event 4 United Bank India Auto-Loan Fraud

Human actions

Lead interviews with implicated field agents and coordinate law-enforcement filings.

Engage external forensic-accounting and public-relations firms, approving budgets and statements.

Submit the 90-day show-cause response to regulators and testify at follow-up hearings if required.

HDT actions

Execute SQL joins across application, collateral, and payment tables to surface duplicate chassis numbers and secondary-loan patterns.

Apply anomaly-detection rules to rank suspect agent IDs and quantify total exposure.

Retrieve RBI circulars and Ministry directives that define reporting format and penalty structure.

Generate a detailed impact report, a blacklist update script for the core lending platform, and a draft regulatory response packet for human legal review.

The interaction paths shown in the sample HDT specification agent calls, peer exchanges, and upward reporting illustrate one possible pattern rather than a universal blueprint. In practice, every enterprise must establish its own communication lattice at the architecture stage, long before any lines of code or prompt templates are written. Factors such as organizational size, geographic reach, regulatory burden, risk tolerance, and data-platform maturity all shape how many HDTs are deployed, where they sit in the hierarchy, and which agents they are permitted to invoke. A regional mid-market company with a single payroll database might pair one payroll HDT with a handful of validation agents, whereas a multinational with dozens of payroll engines, varied tax rules, and multiple unions could justify separate HDTs for hourly, salaried, expatriate, and union payroll, each with distinct peer-to-peer channels and escalation ladders.

Existing human workflows also drive configuration choices. If an organization already relies on decentralized payroll teams, mirroring that model in the digital layer preserves familiarity and eases adoption. In contrast, a highly centralized finance function may opt for one aggregate HDT that validates inputs from all business units and communicates exclusively with a single human payroll hub. Data-governance policy is another constraint: some firms require that only humans view raw personally identifiable information, meaning their HDTs must operate on tokenized data and escalate any record requiring direct PII inspection. Others allow HDTs broader visibility but mandate deeper audit trails, steering architecture toward added logging endpoints and more granular role-based keys.

Budget and talent availability influence responsibility boundaries as well. Organizations with limited AI engineering support may keep HDTs narrow, focused on repetitive validation tasks, while retaining variance analysis and reporting in human hands. Those that can fund larger teams might build multi-layered HDT clusters that pass work among themselves before a single human sees the result, reducing manual touchpoints but demanding stricter orchestration logic. Service-level expectations matter too: if payroll data must be checked within minutes of each feed arriving, architects may add redundant HDTs running in parallel for resilience; where overnight windows are acceptable, a single HDT instance can suffice.

Compliance overhead varies by industry and jurisdiction, further altering the shape of the digital workforce. A pharmaceutical company subject to Good Clinical Practice guidelines and Sarbanes-Oxley will impose heavier segregation-of-duties controls than a privately held retailer. That difference can translate into distinct reporting trees: the pharma payroll HDT might escalate to an HDT compliance officer before finance, whereas the retailer's HDT reports straight to the payroll manager.

Given these variables, the example structure offered here should be considered a starting point a conceptual scaffold to spark internal design workshops, not a plug-and-play template. Each organization must inventory its own regulatory obligations, cultural norms, process dependencies, and technical assets, then draft a bespoke HDT charter that defines tasks, exclusions, agent triggers, and escalation gates. Skipping this exercise risks mismatched responsibilities, audit gaps, and user frustration once the system goes live.

In conclusion, settling HDT counts, scopes, and interaction routes at the architecture phase is essential. Only by grounding the design in real-world operating conditions can a firm capture the efficiency gains of digital labor without compromising accuracy, oversight, or employee trust.

Bringing It All Together: Practical Approaches to AI Implementation

While Data Engineering, AI Agents, and Human Digital Twins are powerful pillars on their own, their real worth emerges only when they work together as a single, well-coordinated structure. Data Engineering supplies certified reference points: Agents transform those points into specific elements such as validated overtime totals or verified premium rates; HDTs interpret the elements in context, recognize when to escalate, and narrate outcomes in language people understand. No single pillar can shoulder the entire load. An Agent that lacks grounded knowledge drifts into guesswork; an HDT without reliable Agents spends time rechecking everything manually; raw data with no twin or Agent stays dormant. Architecture therefore must weave every hand-off so that each pillar lights up exactly when its contribution is needed and then hands the baton cleanly to the next.

A disciplined architecture favors modest, clearly scoped units over sprawling modules. Each Agent should do one thing exceptionally well retrieve benefit premiums, reconcile time-clock entries, confirm tax-table currency rather than juggle several unrelated routines that increase test burden and blur accountability. The same restraint belongs in the HDT layer. A Payroll Twin designed for deduction validation should not also resolve workplace grievances or author compensation policy. Narrow boundaries make logs easy to read, defects easy to trace, and upgrades easy to ship. Spreading responsibility across several compact Twins and Agents may look like more moving parts, yet it actually reduces brittleness and shrinks mean-time-to-repair when something changes.

Enterprises sometimes crave a grand, all-knowing construct that promises to solve every issue with one call. History shows that approach drifts toward fragility. Monolithic payroll suites and one-stop supply-chain platforms often forced organizations to contort long-standing procedures to fit whatever screens and table layouts came out of the box. The result was extra headcount devoted to work-arounds, shadow spreadsheets for edge cases, and years of change-management overhead. Modern language models and modular orchestration let us flip that script. A small Agent can wrap a legacy pension API; a compact HDT can learn a local union agreement without any need to replace the entire payroll core. The system bends to the business, not the other way around.

Mapping real-world outcomes first, not model capabilities guards against technological waste. Architects begin by listing what the organization truly must achieve: employees paid accurately and on time, regulators satisfied that filings are correct, managers able to spot cost variances early. From each outcome they trace back to the data points, cross-checks, and approvals required. Only after this exercise are tasks assigned. If the map shows that a new hire's deduction setup requires eight field verifications, an Agent receives that exact brief. If judgment around a sensitive retroactive pay case is unavoidable, that branch stays with a human supervisor no matter how tempting it might be to automate.

Careful planning also anticipates change. When a new tax rule lands or a benefit plan rolls out midyear, architects can swap a single Agent or adjust one HDT escalation trigger without touching dozens of unrelated modules. Logs remain consistent, error surfaces stay narrow, and regulatory reviewers can follow an uninterrupted story from raw data to final approval.

Focusing on business primacy, modest component size, and pillar interdependence will not deliver overnight miracles. It will, however, produce an AI system that ages gracefully, scales at a pace the organization can absorb, and returns value greater than its maintenance cost. A deliberate, needs-first approach ensures that Data Engineering, Agents, and HDTs function as partners in a living, adaptable framework rather than as isolated showcases of what technology happens to make possible.

Architecting and launching an AI program is not a project that a single data-science or automation team can shoulder alone. Every functional unit, not just IT must help decide how Data Engineering, Agents, and Human Digital Twins come together, because each pillar touches long-standing workflows, regulatory controls, and human relationships. When the planning table excludes payroll, benefits, finance, compliance, or security stakeholders, hidden assumptions creep in and later explode as rework, scope creep, or audit gaps. Successful initiatives invite product owners, process SMEs, risk officers, and workforce representatives to co-author the blueprint, ensuring every pillar lines up with practical realities rather than theoretical convenience.

Below is a non-exhaustive set of considerations that should guide an organization-wide planning session before the first line of code or prompt template is drafted:

- **Explicit Metadata Ownership:** Business leaders not only data architects must claim stewardship of metadata, because the twin and the Agents rely on semantic meaning, not just data types. AI has to know that the column labeled "Plan_Code" in one source maps to "Benefit_Plan_ID" in another, and that a value of "XYZ" signifies a premium deduction, not a retirement match. This richer, business-defined metadata prevents the language model from stitching together mismatched fields or inventing mappings on the fly.
- **Business-Led HDT Definition:** HDT structures should emerge from the ways real people work, rather than forcing every twin through a one-size-fits-all YAML mold. Finance may need a highly detailed variance-analysis twin, while supply chain might rely on a simpler inventory-reconciliation twin. Teams must feel free to add or omit blocks, adjust escalation logic, and embed domain-specific references so the twin mirrors actual tasks.
- **Rich Agent Input for Technical Agents:** When designing a technical Agent such as one that generates SQL or enforces RBAC the specification must supply table names, schema nuances, valid joins, and any row-level security rules. Language models will write code only as accurate as the instructions provided. If column definitions or credential scopes are missing, the Agent will guess, and those guesses turn into broken queries or access violations. Invest the time up front to deliver complete and precise context.
- **Granular Domain Agent Segmentation:** Domain Agents should remain narrowly scoped benefit-rate lookup separate from garnishment policy, sales-commission logic separate from overtime compliance. Combining dissimilar processes in one Agent breeds conflicting rules and hampers troubleshooting. Business involvement is crucial here, because only process experts can outline the subtle boundaries that matter when policies overlap.
- **Data Engineering Is Not Mere ETL:** Moving data from point A to point B doesn't qualify as Data Engineering in an AI context. The engineering layer must catalog every data source, annotate quality gates, reconcile conflicting records, and expose that harmonized view in a manner that AI models can consume without risking duplicate or stale values. A thoughtful layer avoids wholesale data duplication; it focuses on indexing, semantic tagging, and policy-aware access so downstream Agents and HDTs always see a trustworthy version of the truth.
- **Preservation of Existing Investments:** Organizations already own payroll engines, benefits platforms, ERP systems, and compliance tools designed by domain specialists. An AI layer's first responsibility is to work with these proven assets, relieving repetitive work, surfacing gaps, and linking processes, not eclipsing entire platforms. Claims that AI will fully replace a mature, audited payroll system or a specialized tax engine should face rigorous cost-benefit scrutiny, regulatory review, and contingency planning. Where replacement does

occur, the project must be labeled atypical and should proceed only after demonstrating clear, long-term advantage that outweighs risk.

- **Manual-Heavy Process Replacement:** When an organization does choose to retire a system, the candidate will almost always be a spreadsheet-driven, error-prone manual workflow. Automating such tasks with AI yields immediate accuracy gains without jeopardizing high-value domain knowledge or audited functionality. Even then, the decision must reference a measured business case that details operational savings, error reduction, and employee-experience improvements.
- **Continuous Governance Alignment:** Governance committees must monitor pillar interaction from proof-of-concept to production. As new regulations appear or roles shift, metadata owners, Agent maintainers, and HDT designers must adapt together. Skipping governance checkpoints yields brittle point solutions that break under the next tax-law update or organizational restructure.
- **Clear Escalation Protocols:** Each HDT needs an escalation matrix that names human approvers for data gaps, sentiment triggers, or policy ambiguities. LSafety depends on these gates: without them, the twin will either act on incomplete data or flood managers with unnecessary alerts. Balanced thresholds, tuned in consultation with process owners, keep signal and noise in healthy proportion.

Consulting these factors during architecture avoids the trap of "technology first, business later." Enterprises spent decades bending human processes to fit monolithic software suites. The flexible nature of modern AI frameworks reverses that relationship: business logic dictates structure, and the tech layers adapt. Agents become disposable wrappers around legacy APIs; HDTs inherit company-specific procedures rather than imposing vendor defaults; Data Engineering refines meaning rather than simply shifting data.

An organization that embraces this mindset builds a digital workforce that grows organically with shifting market conditions. When a new tax rule arrives, only the tax-calculation Agent changes. If headcount freezes demand more automation, additional HDTs spin up to manage labor-intensive validations, leaving core policy intact. Conversely, if executive leadership decides to replace a niche tool, they do so with eyes open, labeling the move exceptional and validating that AI can meet or exceed the specialized function's safeguards and accuracy levels.

Ultimately, business-first architecture, shared responsibility for metadata, and minimalist, purpose-built Agents and HDTs produce an AI ecosystem that delivers measurable value without sacrificing control or transparency. A meticulous design process ensures each pillar data, automation, and digital cognition contributes exactly what the organization needs, no more and no less, leading to sustainable gains instead of short-lived excitement.

Beyond technical architecture and rigorous system training, effective organization-wide perception management is critical to the successful deployment and adoption of enterprise AI. The most advanced AI technology or meticulous design can still falter if internal stakeholders users, managers, auditors, and leadership do not perceive its introduction positively or clearly understand its intended role. Effective communication around the scope, purpose, boundaries, and expected outcomes of AI implementation is essential. Misaligned perceptions often stem from misunderstandings about AI capabilities, fears around job security, or unrealistic expectations set by sensationalized industry reports or overly ambitious vendor claims. Without proactively shaping these perceptions, even carefully designed AI implementations risk resistance, underutilization, or active circumvention.

AI is not a silver bullet. Organizations must internalize that AI, while powerful, cannot instantly resolve deep-rooted process inefficiencies, poor data management practices, or structural policy ambiguities. The temptation to see AI as an automatic solution to complex organizational problems must be avoided. If the underlying data is inconsistent, incomplete, or unreliable, AI will simply surface these flaws more quickly, potentially magnifying existing issues. Likewise, unclear business rules, poorly defined processes, or ambiguous roles within the organization cannot be magically fixed by AI; rather, such foundational problems must first be addressed. Organizations that believe implementing AI alone can bypass the need for disciplined process improvement or data governance will ultimately face disappointment and wasted investment. AI is best viewed as a powerful enhancement to well-structured and documented processes, not a standalone remedy for chronic organizational challenges.

User interactions must be precisely targeted; prompts and user requests should not be all-encompassing but carefully scoped to the task at hand. AI models rely fundamentally on clear, specific prompts to deliver accurate, reliable, and meaningful results. Broad, generalized requests that attempt to address multiple unrelated topics simultaneously confuse the model, reduce the clarity of its output, and increase the likelihood of generating ambiguous or incorrect responses. For example, an employee asking an HDT to simultaneously summarize payroll variances, propose policy adjustments, and analyze benefits data across multiple locations in a single query will almost certainly lead to poor-quality outcomes. Organizations must train users to formulate requests in precise, manageable segments, aligning each query to a specific HDT or Agent capability. This targeted approach significantly improves AI response accuracy, enhances user satisfaction, and reduces operational risks from overly generalized AI outputs.

Proper training on what constitutes enterprise AI and what does not is critical. Generalized tools like ChatGPT, while powerful and impressive, are not inherently enterprise AI solutions. These public-facing language models draw upon broad, uncontrolled data from across the internet, operate without transparent knowledge grounding or clearly defined business logic, and lack rigorous enterprise security controls or data governance frameworks. Users accustomed to publicly available chat interfaces may mistakenly believe that similar behavior, capabilities, and flexibility apply directly to internal enterprise use cases. This misconception can lead to unrealistic expectations or unsafe behaviors, such as sharing sensitive organizational data with public interfaces. Thus, comprehensive internal training programs must delineate enterprise-specific AI characteristics clearly, emphasizing that real enterprise AI is strictly controlled, utilizes curated, secure, and validated data, and always remains compliant with internal security and regulatory standards.

Strategies to avoid hallucinations situations where AI models generate plausible-sounding but factually incorrect information must be explicitly defined and communicated. Organizations should implement rigorous data-grounding protocols, detailed metadata definitions, and structured prompting strategies designed specifically to constrain model outputs to verified and trusted sources. Additional layers such as fact-checking Agents, cross-validation of outputs, and ongoing monitoring mechanisms significantly reduce hallucination risks. Organizations must educate users explicitly about this phenomenon, teaching them to recognize outputs that seem suspiciously confident yet lack source verification or supporting evidence. Continuous user awareness training is critical to minimizing acceptance of hallucinatory outputs, reinforcing a culture of skepticism, and maintaining vigilance in verifying AI-generated information.

Choosing appropriate LLM AI models is crucial because different processes and activities require distinct reasoning capabilities; no one-size-fits-all LLM strategy adequately addresses every business scenario. Certain processes, such as financial reconciliations, regulatory compliance reviews, or legal interpretations, demand highly specialized reasoning skills, extensive factual grounding, and explicit domain training. Conversely, tasks like general internal policy inquiries or employee communications may be well-served by more flexible or general-purpose language models. A mismatch between model capabilities and the actual reasoning requirements of the process will lead to poor-quality outcomes, compliance breaches, or unnecessarily complicated model tuning efforts. Organizations should adopt a nuanced model-selection strategy, matching model types carefully to specific processes based on explicit reasoning and data-grounding requirements. This tailored approach ensures consistent accuracy, operational reliability, and appropriate cost management across diverse organizational use cases.

AI has inherent flexibility to adapt and learn continuously. Therefore, organizations must establish explicit protocols for ongoing learning, fine-tuning, and model enhancement. Creating a clear AI Center of Excellence (CoE) early in the AI journey, ideally at the strategy formulation phase, significantly strengthens long-term adaptability. This CoE serves as a governance body responsible for monitoring AI model performance, analyzing feedback patterns, validating fine-tuning requirements, and coordinating model updates. Explicit protocols for how learning occurs such as which feedback loops are monitored, how training data sets are refreshed, and who approves model adjustments must be documented clearly. Without formalized protocols, organizations risk fragmented updates, duplicated effort, or inconsistent model behavior. Clearly defined CoE governance ensures model improvements align consistently with evolving business requirements and organizational priorities.

Encouraging users to provide feedback objectively and devoid of emotional bias is essential for effective AI model evolution. Subjective, emotionally charged, or unclear feedback can misguide AI model adjustments, leading to unnecessary changes or missed opportunities for genuine improvements. Organizations should implement structured feedback forms or objective rating scales, prompting users to specify precise issues or improvement areas. For example, instead of vague complaints such as "this output is useless," users should be guided toward specific constructive criticisms like "the variance explanation is incomplete because it omits the impact of recent benefit rate changes." Objective feedback ensures clear, actionable improvement insights for model developers, reduces misunderstanding, and accelerates effective fine-tuning. Structured feedback processes also foster a collaborative organizational culture where users see themselves as integral contributors to AI enhancement rather than passive recipients.

Avoiding the temptation to chase AI-related hype is critical. Organizations differ significantly in technological maturity, regulatory environments, industry standards, political climates, and internal readiness for innovation. Just because a certain AI implementation or technology receives extensive industry attention or media coverage does not mean it suits every organization or scenario equally. Adopting technology simply based on its popularity or external pressure often leads to misaligned investment, unmet expectations, or operational disruption. Organizations must carefully assess their unique maturity levels, business objectives, risk tolerance, political climate, and available resources before adopting new technologies. Internal pilot programs, gradual implementation approaches, and rigorous ROI assessments provide reliable safeguards against overly ambitious or mismatched technology investments. Prudently aligning AI strategy with organizational needs rather than external trends significantly enhances long-term adoption success, operational stability, and measurable business benefits.

An additional factor for consideration is transparent communication from executive leadership. Visible executive sponsorship and clearly communicated organizational intentions regarding AI implementations are essential for fostering internal confidence and reducing resistance. Employees who perceive AI initiatives as opaque or unclear are far more likely to resist adoption or undermine initiatives through passive non-engagement. Transparent executive communications must clearly outline strategic intentions, reassure staff about job security and opportunities, and explicitly clarify AI limitations and safeguards. This transparency builds internal trust, supports smoother implementation, and reinforces organizational alignment around clearly understood AI initiatives.

Effective AI implementation extends far beyond technology selection, model training, and data management. Organization-wide perception management and comprehensive internal education are equally critical. Clearly communicating AI's intended role, limitations, and integration into existing business processes fosters user confidence and reduces adoption friction. Avoiding unrealistic expectations, carefully matching AI models to business needs, and cultivating objective feedback mechanisms ensure consistent accuracy and long-term improvement. Establishing clear AI governance through a CoE, maintaining a rigorous learning and fine-tuning protocol, and avoiding external hype further strengthen organizational resilience and adoption success. These meticulous perception management and training strategies ensure enterprise AI initiatives deliver sustained value and meaningful operational improvement.

High Level AI Adoption Strategy Flow

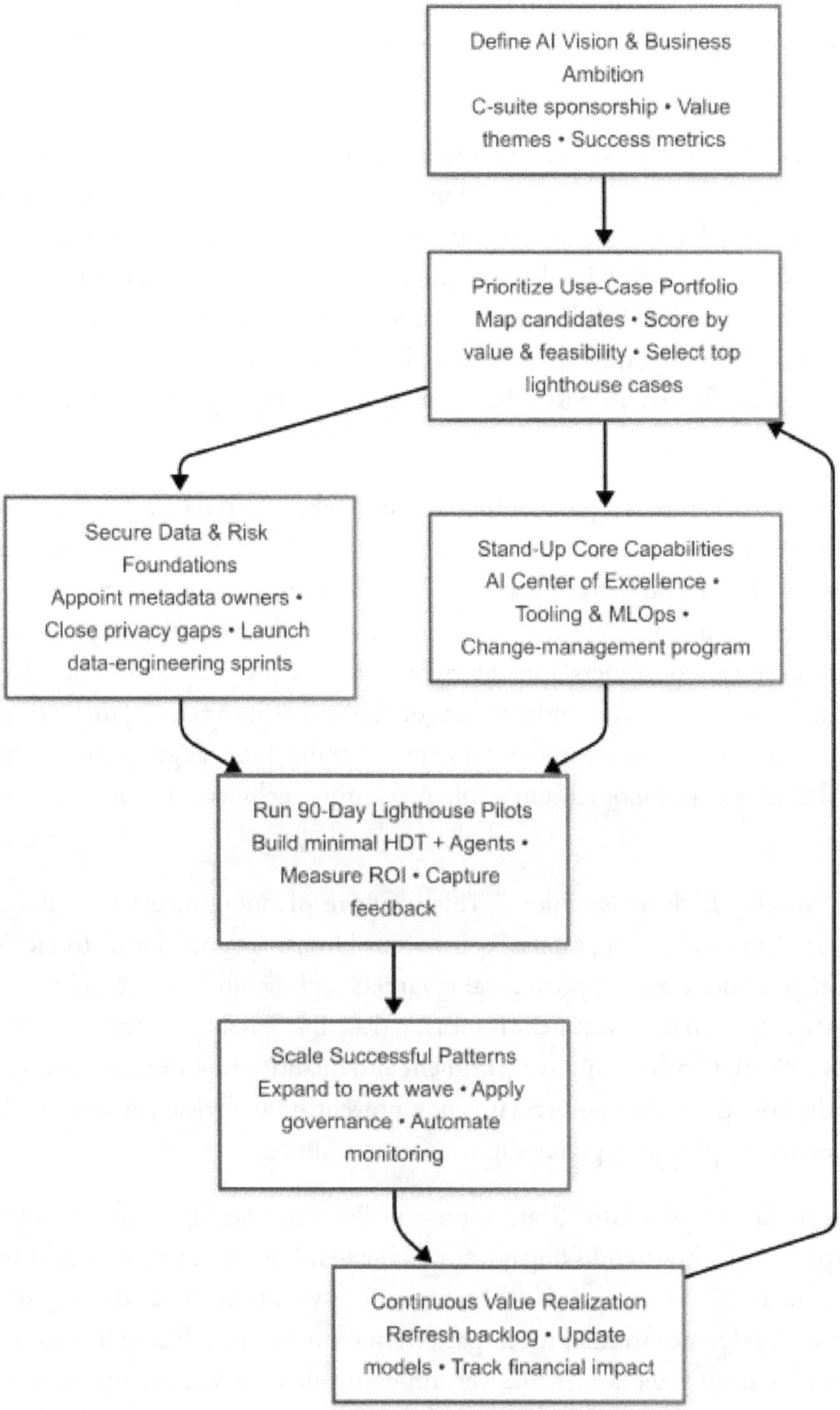

High Level AI Adoption Strategy Flow

The diagram outlines a disciplined, end-to-end pathway for enterprise AI adoption that mirrors a classic strategy-execution cycle yet acknowledges the unique demands of large-language-model implementations. It begins with a squarely strategic phase "Define AI Vision & Business Ambition" because every successful transformation must start with clarity at the top. C-suite sponsorship gives AI programs the political capital and budgetary authority they need to break functional silos, while an explicit value thesis cost efficiency, incremental revenue, better risk control anchors future decisions to outcomes, not hype. Specifying success metrics at this first step heads off the tendency to judge AI by vague promises: if leadership declares "3 percent expense reduction in payroll processing" or "20 percent faster dispute resolution," the organization instantly gains a yardstick for evaluating use-case ideas and technology proposals.

Flow then moves to "Prioritize Use-Case Portfolio." No enterprise has unlimited time or resources to chase every shiny AI opportunity, so this step insists on rigor. Teams cast a wide net, mapping dozens of candidate processes across finance, HR, supply chain, and customer operations. Each candidate is scored on three axes: tangible value it can deliver, technical feasibility given current data maturity, and speed of implementation. The highest-scoring opportunities become "lighthouse cases" small in number but rich enough to validate architectural assumptions, showcase early wins, and build momentum for cultural change. Choosing such lighthouses is not simply a "quick win" hunt; it is a strategic balancing act that reveals integration challenges, establishes realistic ROI baselines, and prototypes governance controls in a safe domain before scale.

Once priorities are set, the roadmap forks intentionally into two parallel foundation tracks. On the left, "Secure Data & Risk Foundations" recognizes that AI cannot run on goodwill and spreadsheets. Metadata owners are appointed so every data element carries a living business definition, and privacy gaps are closed to satisfy regulators. The phrase "data-engineering sprints" signals that datasets will be indexed, cleaned, and semantically tagged so that Agents and HDTs consult only trusted pipelines rather than scattered extracts. On the right, "Stand-Up Core Capabilities" lays organizational plumbing an AI Center of Excellence to codify standards, a tool chain that covers everything from MLOps to RBAC enforcement, and a structured change-management program to train users, align policies, and adapt job roles. Running these tracks in parallel accelerates momentum while preventing technical enthusiasm from outrunning compliance readiness.

Both foundation tracks converge into "Run 90-Day Lighthouse Pilots." This is where planning meets measurable reality. Teams build the minimum viable set of Data Engineering assets, Agents, and Human Digital Twins to tackle each lighthouse use case. Crucially, pilots operate under board-approved value targets and data-privacy guidelines so outcomes translate directly to leadership language. Return on investment is measured against baseline metrics declared in the strategy phase, and rich user feedback is collected both qualitative sentiment and quantitative interaction logs to refine models, prompts, and escalation logic. The 90-day window enforces urgency, preventing analytical paralysis while still allowing enough cycles to identify wrinkles in data pipelines, policy gates, and user training.

After pilots demonstrate repeatable gains, the roadmap flows into "Scale Successful Patterns." Scaling is not a simple matter of copying pilot code across the enterprise; it involves codifying governance, extending metadata stewardship, and automating monitoring so each new Agent or HDT operates under the same visibility and control as the original. New business units or regions are onboarded with reference to the proven pattern book developed during lighthouse execution. Automated model monitoring ensures drift detection, while version-controlled YAML definitions and cataloged data pipelines allow quick rollout without custom coding each instance. Governance committees now have tangible artifacts validated prompts, audit logs, ROI dashboards to standardize adoption while retaining flexibility for unit-specific policy variations.

The diagram loops into "Continuous Value Realization," signaling that AI transformation is not a one-time program but an evergreen discipline. Quarterly backlog refreshes add or retire use cases based on evolving strategy and regulatory changes. Models are retrained on fresh data, fine-tuning parameters are reviewed, and new Agents are integrated as business needs evolve. Financial impact tracking is ongoing; the same KPIs established in the first stage continue to inform resource allocation, keeping the AI engine honest in its promises and transparent in its performance. The arrow that cycles back to "Prioritize Use-Case Portfolio" illustrates this perpetual loop: each wave of deployment informs the next, and lessons learned from production environments become starting assumptions for subsequent ideation cycles.

Collectively, the flow ensures that AI adoption never devolves into isolated proofs of concept or runaway technical experiments. By anchoring every phase to explicit business ambition, measurable metrics, and governance controls, enterprises avoid both the paralysis of endless study and the chaos of uncontrolled experimentation. The two-track foundation approach ensures data, risk, and organizational readiness catch up to, and then pace, technical ambition. Lighthouse pilots provide a crucible where architectural claims are stress-evaluated against real users and real data, while the scaling and continuous-value stages institutionalize successful patterns without ossifying them.

With the long-term roadmap defined, the immediate focus shifts to the 90-day lightning pilot. This concentrated effort turns architectural intent into operational proof by standing up just enough Data Engineering, Agent, and HDT components to tackle the selected lighthouse use case under real conditions. Strict timeboxing forces rapid decision-making, but the pilot is never a throwaway experiment; every model, prompt template, and audit log generated during these three months is designed to roll forward into the broader program. Success is gauged against the value metrics set in the vision stage whether cost savings, cycle-time reduction, or risk mitigation so executives can link outcomes directly to strategic goals. Lessons learned on data quality, user-prompt behavior, and escalation thresholds feed straight back into governance playbooks, ensuring scaling happens on a foundation evaluated by actual users, real workloads, and measurable financial impact.

90 Day Pilot Plan

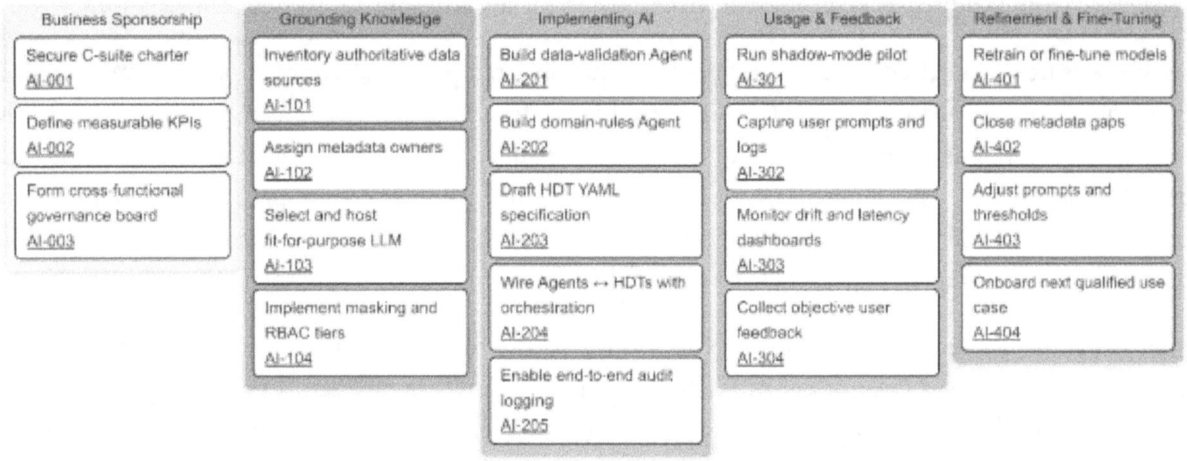

90 Day Pilot Plan

The board displays a full-lifecycle kanban view tailored for an enterprise AI deployment and arranged from left to right to reflect sequential maturity. Each vertical lane groups tasks by phase, highlighting how leadership commitment, data foundations, technical build, user co-creation, and iterative optimization must progress in lock-step rather than in isolation. Cards carry unique identifiers AI-001 through AI-404 so every deliverable can be budgeted, assigned, and tracked in the same ticketing system that governs traditional initiatives; this parity matters because AI projects succeed only when folded into existing portfolio-management disciplines rather than treated as experimental side work.

The first lane, "Business Sponsorship," establishes executive ownership. Securing a C-suite charter (AI-001) creates top-down authority to unlock data sets, allocate budgets, and resolve cross-functional conflicts. Defining measurable KPIs (AI-002) turns lofty ambition into accountable targets, such as "10 percent reduction in payroll processing effort" or "30 percent faster compliance turnaround." Forming a cross-functional governance board (AI-003) institutionalizes decision rights so that risk officers, domain leaders, and technology owners all share stewardship, preventing the AI program from drifting into narrow technical focus while ignoring policy or workforce implications.

"Grounding Knowledge" is the second lane because no AI system whether model, Agent, or HDT outperforms the quality of its input data. Inventorying authoritative data sources (AI-101) forces stewards to enumerate systems of record, shadow files, and external feeds before any development begins; surprises discovered later become far costlier to remediate. Assigning metadata owners (AI-102) means every field "Deduction_Code," "Union_Class," "Overtime_Rate" now has a living business dictionary entry and a named steward who can approve changes or clarify semantics for model fine-tuning. Selecting and hosting a fit-for-purpose LLM (AI-103) happens here, not during development, because model capabilities must align with data-privacy commitments and latency expectations established by business stakeholders. Implementing masking and RBAC tiers (AI-104) closes privacy gaps so sensitive salary or health-benefit data appear only in tokenized form when the HDT consults them; this tactical control mitigates legal exposure while preserving analytical richness.

"Implementing AI" translates business intent and grounded data into operational artifacts. Building the data-validation Agent (AI-201) creates the first guardrail: it ensures missing deductions, inactive bank accounts, or duplicate employee records are flagged before any downstream orchestration. The domain-rules Agent (AI-202) codifies complex regulation union overtime multipliers, garnishment ceilings, locality tax overrides so the HDT can query an authoritative microservice instead of embedding fragile hard-coded rules inside prompts. Drafting the HDT YAML specification (AI-203) captures role narrative, scope boundaries, escalation criteria, and agent-invocation patterns in a format both humans and LLMs can parse consistently. Wiring Agents ↔ HDTs with orchestration logic (AI-204) stitches together asynchronous calls, data caching, and retry semantics that human specialists implicitly manage through experience; explicit orchestration prevents race conditions or double counting when multiple Agents return overlapping data. Audit logging (AI-205) records every query, hash, and reasoning string so external auditors can reconstruct flow, fulfilling the transparency commitments set in KPIs.

The "Usage & Feedback" lane confirms that real users payroll clerks, HR generalists, compliance reviewers can rely on the system. Running shadow-mode pilots (AI-301) lets HDTs and Agents process live data without yet influencing production outcomes, divergences from the human baseline surface improvement opportunities. Capturing user prompts and logs (AI-302) supplies empirical evidence of how employees actually request information, which rarely matches theoretical prompt libraries drafted in isolation. Monitoring drift and latency dashboards (AI-303) offers dynamic insight: if response times lengthen during month-end close or accuracy decays as benefit plans change mid-year, technologists see it quickly rather than weeks later in error reports. Collecting objective feedback (AI-304) cements a culture of constructive critique rather than emotional venting; structured forms channel observations into retrainable signals for model owners, closing the data-science feedback loop.

The final lane, "Refinement & Fine-Tuning," institutionalizes constant evolution so the system never ossifies into a brittle artifact. Retraining or fine-tuning models (AI-401) incorporates new benefit plans, tax changes, or language patterns captured during the previous lane; the Center of Excellence reviews drift metrics and approves updated weights before promotion to production. Closing metadata gaps (AI-402) keeps the business dictionary alive, adding new fields and deprecating obsolete ones uncovered during pilot usage. Adjusting prompts and thresholds (AI-403) tunes escalation sensitivity perhaps lowering the sentiment trigger after discovering too many false irate flags. Finally, onboarding the next qualified use case (AI-404) codifies scaling discipline: only when the prior wave meets its KPIs and governance checks does the backlog release another scenario, ensuring each phase builds on a strong foundation rather than spreading resources thin.

Taken as a whole, the board demonstrates that AI adoption is not a whimsical journey but a managed value chain from strategic charter to continuous learning each task linked to measurable impact, governed data, explicit ownership, and incremental expansion.

Throughout this chapter, it has become evident that the successful adoption of enterprise AI requires a strategic framework and a clearly defined roadmap as foundational prerequisites. Embarking on AI initiatives without such planning exposes organizations to risks of misalignment, inefficiencies, redundancy, and ultimately diminished returns. A comprehensive strategy sets clear expectations across all levels of the organization, aligning business goals with technological execution. It ensures that every stakeholder from executive leadership to operational teams shares a common understanding of what AI intends to achieve, how success will be measured, and what role each individual and team plays in realizing that success.

A well-structured roadmap clarifies crucial aspects such as executive sponsorship, governance mechanisms, resource allocation, risk mitigation strategies, and clearly defined success criteria. This proactive approach helps eliminate ambiguity and confusion by defining specific phases and tasks, delineating responsibilities, and articulating measurable outcomes. As organizations prepare to implement AI technologies, the roadmap serves as a guiding reference that facilitates cross-functional collaboration, ensures data integrity, promotes robust metadata management, and encourages consistent organizational practices. It becomes an essential tool in bridging the gap between ambitious business aspirations and technical execution.

The roadmap approach described reinforces that AI adoption is not a one-time technology deployment but a continuous and iterative discipline requiring sustained focus, commitment, and active governance. It compels organizations to think through critical issues such as data privacy, regulatory compliance, ethics, and ongoing system reliability and maintenance upfront rather than reactively addressing these challenges as they arise. Without strategic foresight, organizations often face fragmented efforts, increased operational friction, costly retracing of steps, and prolonged adoption timelines, thus undermining the fundamental promise of AI.

Organizations equipped with a clearly articulated strategy and execution roadmap can more confidently embark on their AI journey. By understanding and outlining upfront what AI can and cannot do, enterprises position themselves for realistic, sustainable successes rather than fleeting, short-term gains. The roadmap empowers organizations to thoughtfully leverage AI's potential, maintain strategic flexibility, minimize risk, and deliver consistent, meaningful business value aligned with core organizational priorities and long-term objectives.

Conclusion

In this comprehensive exploration of enterprise AI, we embarked on a meticulous journey to demystify, structure, and strategically anchor artificial intelligence within real-world business operations. Rather than approaching AI as simply another technological advancement, we framed it explicitly as a transformative paradigm that enhances human capabilities, enriches organizational knowledge, and delivers quantifiable value. Our core objective has been clear throughout: to provide enterprises not merely with an abstract understanding of AI, but a tangible roadmap to harness its full potential, manage associated risks, and integrate AI thoughtfully into day-to-day processes.

We began by carefully examining the philosophy underpinning AI applications, establishing a foundational perspective that AI's primary role within modern business is to reliably navigate complexity and create order from vast informational chaos. Far from replacing human judgment or removing critical decision-making capabilities from organizational leadership, AI serves as a powerful enabler of structured cognition, allowing companies to uncover purposeful insights, streamline communication, and clarify operational transparency. This philosophical foundation set the stage for a detailed discussion of how enterprises should systematically approach AI adoption not with blind optimism or technological fascination, but with measured deliberation and purposeful alignment to strategic organizational objectives.

Central to this deliberation is the recognition that successful AI integration depends on the interconnected strengths of three critical pillars: Data Engineering (Grounded Knowledge), AI Agents, and Human Digital Twins (HDTs). Each pillar was carefully explored, detailed, and illustrated, underscoring their distinctive yet interdependent roles. Data Engineering emerged clearly as the essential foundation the rigorous process of identifying, organizing, and tagging structured and unstructured data in ways that enable AI systems to access and interpret it accurately and consistently. Far more than mere data migration or traditional ETL processes, this pillar establishes semantic clarity, prevents AI hallucinations, and ensures accuracy in all downstream analyses and decisions.

AI Agents, positioned clearly within this structure, were articulated as specialized digital assistants precisely scoped entities capable of executing predefined tasks with remarkable consistency and speed. Rather than broadly scoped "black box" agents, we emphasized the necessity of narrowly tailored and carefully architected agents, each explicitly aligned to specific tasks such as SQL query execution, validation checks, security enforcement, or regulatory compliance monitoring. This meticulous design strategy ensures transparency, simplifies audits, and guarantees clarity in agent outputs, reinforcing trust and reliability across all organizational functions.

The concept of Human Digital Twins provided a deeply nuanced perspective, recognizing that while AI can replicate structured cognitive processes, it cannot authentically emulate human emotional intelligence or nuanced situational judgment. HDTs were therefore depicted not as replacements for human professionals, but as complementary digital colleagues, capable of reliably managing routine interactions, escalating emotionally charged inquiries, and ensuring procedural integrity. Through detailed discussion and illustrative examples, it became clear that precisely defined roles and unambiguous escalation pathways are critical to the successful integration of HDTs within existing organizational hierarchies and workflows.

The chapters dedicated to practical implementation reinforced a fundamental truth: that successful enterprise AI adoption does not happen through isolated technical projects but through coordinated organizational alignment, disciplined strategic governance, and clearly defined roadmaps. We detailed the importance of executive sponsorship, clearly articulated success criteria, robust metadata management, tailored model selection, comprehensive feedback mechanisms, and continuous refinement processes. By carefully framing each implementation phase, we underscored that genuine AI transformation requires thoughtful orchestration across business sponsorship, knowledge grounding, careful agent and HDT design, controlled user engagement, and iterative fine-tuning.

Moreover, we devoted substantial attention to organizational perception management, dispelling misconceptions, addressing unrealistic expectations, and underscoring that AI is neither a universal panacea nor a threat to human roles. We emphasized targeted, focused user interactions with AI, rather than broad, ambiguous inquiries. Detailed strategies to prevent AI hallucinations by maintaining strong grounding practices, clear prompt management, and stringent validation processes were presented as essential safeguards. Furthermore, the necessity of selecting appropriate Large Language Models (LLMs) tailored explicitly to organizational requirements was clearly highlighted, recognizing that one-size-fits-all approaches rarely deliver optimal outcomes.

The practical application of AI was thoroughly illustrated through realistic scenarios, including payroll inquiry processes within medium and large enterprises. These scenarios demonstrated concretely how AI pillars integrate seamlessly, how clear escalation paths and specialized agent roles simplify complexity, and how meticulous AI architecture dramatically enhances accuracy, reduces manual workloads, and consistently delivers organizational value. These examples served not merely as theoretical exercises but as compelling evidence that disciplined, structured AI implementation carefully aligned with organizational scale and operational complexity can deliver sustained, measurable benefits.

The final sections emphasized the necessity of structured strategic planning before AI implementation. An articulated roadmap and strategic vision are essential to ensuring organizational coherence, clarity, and alignment of resources, particularly given the transformative implications of AI across an enterprise. Rather than simply adopting AI out of perceived necessity or market-driven urgency, we argued compellingly for strategic discipline, clearly defined milestones, measurable KPIs, rigorous governance practices, and strong executive leadership. A clearly defined roadmap provides organizations with crucial mechanisms to track progress, evaluate performance, manage risk, ensure regulatory compliance, and avoid pitfalls common to poorly planned technology initiatives.

Concluding this extensive examination, the central message is abundantly clear: artificial intelligence represents an unprecedented opportunity for enterprises to streamline operations, enhance decision accuracy, and extend human expertise into domains of complexity and scale previously unimaginable. Yet, realizing AI's transformative potential requires more than technological enthusiasm or superficial experimentation it demands an unwavering commitment to thoughtful planning, rigorous architecture, precise execution, and continuous organizational learning. Only organizations that approach AI deliberately, transparently, and systematically, with a clearly articulated philosophy, robust governance structures, meticulous data foundations, carefully constructed agent capabilities, nuanced digital twin design, and consistent user feedback mechanisms, will truly unlock AI's fullest potential.

Ultimately, the journey toward sustainable AI adoption is a continuous cycle of clarity, execution, refinement, and growth. AI implementation is never truly finished; rather, it evolves in step with organizational maturity, shifting business priorities, and dynamic market conditions. As enterprises successfully integrate AI into their fabric through rigorous methodologies, strategic foresight, disciplined implementation, and continuous refinement they position themselves not only to excel in the present but to adapt proactively to future opportunities and challenges. The principles, frameworks, and detailed guidance provided throughout this work are intended to empower enterprises to navigate this transformative journey confidently, systematically, and sustainably, delivering lasting competitive advantage, operational excellence, and meaningful human-centered value.

In a time and age where the hype surrounding artificial intelligence often surpasses genuine understanding, the gap between expectation and reality can pose significant challenges to meaningful adoption. Throughout history, humanity has witnessed transformative innovations fire, the printing press, electricity, computers, and the internet each fundamentally reshaping society, expanding human capability, and redefining the boundaries of civilization. AI, in its fullest and most responsible realization, stands poised to join this elite echelon of revolutionary advancements, profoundly enhancing our collective intelligence and decision-making capacity. Its promise is to bring clarity to complexity, consistency to ambiguity, and accuracy to uncertainty, enabling human professionals to transcend limitations in processing vast amounts of information, interpreting intricate patterns, and deriving purposeful meaning from seemingly chaotic data.

Yet, the very excitement surrounding artificial intelligence threatens to become its greatest obstacle. When sensationalized expectations collide with early implementation realities unstructured data, unclear governance, misaligned strategies, or immature technology the inevitable gap between promise and delivery can lead to skepticism, frustration, and ultimately, disillusionment. The risk is not merely that individual AI projects may falter; rather, that entire organizations may prematurely lose confidence in AI's transformative potential. Overhyped narratives, fueled by speculative projections and overly ambitious claims, risk obscuring the tangible, incremental gains AI can reliably deliver when implemented thoughtfully, patiently, and meticulously.

Therefore, the key to harnessing AI's genuine potential lies in disciplined expectation management, realistic target-setting, and rigorous strategic execution. Organizations must resist the temptation to pursue superficial, headline-grabbing AI initiatives; instead, they should adopt deliberate, focused approaches that emphasize grounded knowledge, precise agent design, thoughtful human-digital collaboration, and continuous refinement through measurable, practical results. Responsible adoption requires clear-eyed acknowledgment of both AI's profound strengths and its real limitations, ensuring that the technology is viewed as a supportive collaborator rather than an omnipotent, magical solution.

Ultimately, the true potential of artificial intelligence transcends technological sophistication or computational power alone. Its deepest value is realized when it becomes seamlessly integrated into human workflows, enriching human judgment, enhancing human accuracy, and empowering human professionals. By systematically leveraging AI's capacity to manage routine, repetitive, and data-intensive tasks, organizations free their people to focus on uniquely human endeavors innovation, empathy, creativity, and strategic insight thus amplifying rather than diminishing human agency.

In conclusion, the journey toward meaningful AI adoption demands wisdom, patience, strategic discipline, and humility recognizing clearly that AI, at its core, is a powerful human invention designed to extend and amplify human intelligence, not replace it. By navigating the current hype-driven landscape with caution, rigor, and responsible planning, enterprises can ensure that AI reaches its full transformative potential, creating lasting, sustainable value for society. To achieve this, organizations must look beyond sensational headlines and short-term hype cycles, committing instead to the disciplined pursuit of incremental, transparent, and measurable progress.

If AI is embraced thoughtfully, carefully, and purposefully, it can indeed become one of humanity's defining innovations enhancing our civilization's collective intelligence, reshaping how we work, communicate, and innovate, and equipping us to confront challenges that currently exceed our capabilities. However, if we succumb to hype and superficiality, treating AI as a fleeting trend rather than a fundamental paradigm shift, we risk forfeiting this extraordinary opportunity, leaving our organizations and civilization itself poorer for the missed potential.

Thus, the imperative for today's leaders and innovators is clear: approach AI not merely with enthusiasm, but with deep intellectual honesty and strategic clarity. Only then can artificial intelligence fulfill its genuine promise becoming a powerful, enduring enabler of human potential, an essential partner in our shared pursuit of knowledge, clarity, and progress, and ultimately, a defining force in shaping a more intelligent, resilient, and prosperous civilization.

Conclusion

fundae University, university.fundae.ai[1]

fundae.university@fundae.ai

1. http://www.fundae.ai

www.ingramcontent.com/pod-product-compliance
Lightning Source LLC
LaVergne TN
LVHW082350200926
848481LV00012B/3517
9798231098552